SUPPORTING
EVERY CHILD

SU
EV

r
s
d
g

's
n
d

First published in 2009 by Learning Matters Ltd

British Library Cataloguing in Publication Data
A CIP record for this book is available from the British Library.

ISBN: 978 1 84445 203 3

Cover design by Topics
Text design by Bob Rowinski (Code 5)
Project Management by Diana Chambers
Typeset by Kelly Gray
Printed and bound in Great Britain by TJ International Ltd, Padstow, Cornwall
Learning Matters Ltd
33 Southernhay East
Exeter EX1 1NX
Tel: 01392 215560

info@learningmatters.co.uk
www.learningmatters.co.uk

FSC
Mixed Sources
Product group from well-managed
forests and other controlled sources

Cert no. SGS-COC-2482
www.fsc.org
© 1996 Forest Stewardship Council

Contents

Editors and contributors

Anita Walton

Anita Walton is Head of Undergraduate Professional Development at Edge Hill University. In this role she is responsible for Professional Development provision for Support staff and the wider school workforce. Anita was a secondary school teacher and also has extensive experience of teaching on Foundation Degrees for teaching assistants and for the wider school workforce. In addition, Anita has experience as Programme Leader for the Foundation Degree in Supporting Teaching and Learning.

Gillian Goddard

Gillian's experience includes Course Leader for the BA (Hons) in Teaching, Learning and Mentoring at Edge Hill University. In this role she promoted, interviewed and monitored recruitment and retention on this degree programme, monitoring and assuring quality of product and outcomes and student experiences. She currently teaches on the Foundation Degree in Supporting Teaching and Learning and also PHSE modules for Initial Teacher Training.

Jean Bedford

With a background in Primary Education, Jean is currently a senior lecturer at Edge Hill University and has extensive experience of teaching on Foundation Degrees for teaching assistants and also as an assessor for Higher Level Teaching Assistants. Her other roles include teaching on the Foundation Degree for Professional Development, teaching on the BA (Hons) with QTS and supervising students preparing their dissertations. In addition Jean has experience as Primary Pathway Leader on the Foundation Degree in Supporting Teaching and Learning.

Karen Castle

Karen Castle is the Shropshire Manager for Edge Hill University, based in Shrewsbury, Shropshire. She has currently been the Cheshire Co-ordinator for Edge Hill, and prior to that, she was a manager in further education. Karen has experience in management within areas of the public sector, in particular health and social care. Her current role is focused on the management and co-ordination of the university outreach centre in Shropshire, this involves accrediting CPD programmes for the whole school workforce.

Vicky Duckworth

Vicky is Course Leader for the full-time programme in Post-Compulsory Education and Training at Edge Hill University. She is also Research Associate at the Centre for Learning Identity Studies. She is passionate about the empowering and transforming nature of education and keen to establish and maintain strong and productive links between research and practice.

Linda Dunne

Linda Dunne began her career in education as an English teacher working in mainstream and special schools. She now works as a Lecturer in undergraduate and postgraduate professional development programmes in the area of inclusive education and as an Associate Fellow in the Faculty of Education at Edge Hill University.

Susan Faragher

Following many years as a teacher in a Primary school and two years as a Local Authority Adviser, Sue is now the Edge Hill University Outreach Centre Manager based in Wirral LA. She has responsibility for promoting and marketing professional development for both undergraduate and postgraduate colleagues in Wirral Local Authority and the academic responsibility for the students engaged in either work based or taught modules. Sue is currently studying for an Educational Doctorate and has extensive experience of teaching on the Foundation Degrees for Teaching Assistants, Early Years Professional Status and the Masters Degree in Education.

Sue Farrimond

Sue Farrimond is currently working as Head of ITT Partnership at Edge Hill University. Previously she worked as a, teacher in Knowsley, starting her career as a NQT in English and Drama and finally working as an Assistant Head Teacher with responsibility for Learning and Teaching and working as a practitioner research consultant for the local authority. Her main areas of research interest are learner voice and ownership of learning.

Susan Graves

Sue Graves is Programme Leader in the Faculty of Education at Edge Hill University, for the BA (Hons) and Foundation Degree in Professional Development. Sue teaches on programmes and professional development courses for those in non-teaching roles within schools and also on the Masters Degree Programme for teachers in schools. Her research interests include, developing the wider school workforce, using action learning, developing reflective practice, developing learner identity and e-learning to improve access to learning.

Maureen Judge

Maureen has extensive experience as a primary school teacher and also in higher education as Programme Leader for a Foundation degree for teaching assistants. She currently is primary pathway leader for the Foundation Degree in Supporting Teaching and Learning and also teaches on Initial Teacher Training Programmes in Mathematics Primary Education.

Elizabeth Kirtlan

Elizabeth Kirtlan is a senior lecturer working on the Foundation Degree for Supporting, Teaching and Learning. She has experience of working with teaching assistants on this degree. She is also an experienced Primary School teacher who has extensive knowledge of the different roles of teaching assistants in school settings.

Alexis Moore

Alexis Moore is a Senior Lecturer in the Faculty of Education and former Headteacher of a Primary School. Her main teaching role is with support staff on foundation degrees and the development of work-based learning modules. She is active within the Faculty of Education in providing opportunities for wider participation and access to Higher Education for support staff in educational settings. Her research interests include the development of roles and CPD within the Children's Workforce.

Felix Obadan

Felix Obadan is Course Leader for the PGCE Mathematics flexible programme at Edge Hill University. He is a senior lecturer and has worked with teaching Assistants from both primary and secondary schools for eight years. During this period, he coordinated the Maths and Science pilot training programme for Teaching Assistants in the North-West of England on behalf of the Training and Development Agency for schools (TDA). He is also experienced in teaching modules around the wider school workforce.

Joanne Sutcliffe

Joanne worked as a classroom teacher for three years before leaving to work with adults at further education, supporting adult literacy and numeracy. She has since worked within Higher Education for over five years and is Programme Leader for the Foundation Degree in Supporting Teaching and Learning. During this time she has taught a variety of subjects to students on the degree both face to face and online. As part of her MA degree she examined specific learning difficulties as part of this.

PART 1
EVERY CHILD MATTERS

1 INTRODUCTION: THE CONTEXT OF THE *EVERY CHILD MATTERS* AGENDA AND ITS RELEVANCE TO SUPPORT STAFF

Anita Walton and Gillian Goddard

CHAPTER OBJECTIVES

By the end of this chapter you will:

- know what the *Every Child Matters* (ECM) agenda is;

- recognise the impact of this agenda on education provision and practice, now and in the future;

- recognise the role of support staff in the implementation the ECM agenda;

- be able to identify the potential constraints on full implementation of the ECM agenda in educational settings.

LINKS TO **HLTA** STANDARDS

1. Have high expectations of children and young people with a commitment to helping them fulfil their potential.

2. Establish fair, respectful, trusting, supportive and constructive relationships with children and young people.

3. Improve their own knowledge and practice.

4. Understand the key factors that affect children's and young people's learning and progress.

5. Know how other frameworks, which support the development and well-being of children and young people, impact upon their practice.

6. Recognise and respond appropriately to situations that challenge equality of opportunity.

Introduction

The Every Child Matters agenda

The British government's green paper, *Every Child Matters* (DfES, 2003a) was published as part of a cross-departmental response to the Victoria Climbié Inquiry findings. It identified four key themes for change.

1. Increasing the focus on supporting families and carers because they are critical to each child's life.
2. Ensuring necessary intervention before children reach crisis point and protecting children from 'falling through the net' of child protection agencies and procedures.
3. Addressing the underlying problems of weak acountability and poor integration of agency information.
4. Ensuring that staff who work with children are valued, rewarded and trained, hitherto an area of extreme neglect.

(adapted from DCSF, 2008b, p1)

The green paper prompted an extraordinary amount of debate because it had chosen to take so revolutionary a look at services for children, rather than focus, as it had done previously, on individual agency failings. The breadth and depth of the changes it proposed would impact on every agency involved with the delivery of services for children, including the National Health Service, police, local authority administration and management, education, social services and youth justice provision.

Following consultation, the government proceeded to implement its aims and provisions through the law in the Children Act 2004 and by a policy document, 'Every child matters: change for children' (November 2004). It planned a series of reforms over a ten-year period, several of which are still being implemented as part of a phased development.

Aims

The aims of this policy were all encompassing. It proposed that there would be a new approach to ensuring that, from birth to the age of 19, the well-being of all children and young people would be realised. It identified five key outcomes in this respect, which all agencies involved in working with or supporting children should adopt as central to their provision. As the government articulated, the aim is:

> *that every child, whatever their background or their circumstances, will have the support they need to:*
> * *Be healthy*
> * *Stay safe*
> * *Enjoy and achieve*
> * *Make a positive contribution*
> * *Achieve economic well-being.*

(DCSF, 2008b, p1)

Integration of services

One of the key strategies implemented through this was the integration of service provision, a notoriously difficult area that had proved highly resistant to change. Undaunted, the government inplemented over 150 local change strategies that demanded improved integration of *front-line, processes, strategy and governance* (DCSF, 2008b, p1). It produced the famous 'onion' model (Figure 1.1) for whole-system change.

Figure 1.1: 'Onion' model for whole-system change.

The government started this change top-down with the reform of governance. The Department for Education and Skills (DfES) became renamed and merged into the Department for Children, Schools and Families (DCSF), shifting the focus of the department from education to comprehensive child provision. Local education authorities were abolished and replaced with local authority children services, which had responsibility for all services involving childen that were provided by local authorities.

Children's Trusts

The local authority is also a member of the local Children's Trust. These were set up in 2005 to promote children's and young people's well-being and to ensure that the legislative *duty to cooperate* (Children Act 2004) between key children's services providers was fulfilled and facilitated. The essential features of a Children's Trust are, according to the official *Every Child Matters* website, as follows.

- *Outcome-led vision (which means that they need to secure improved results determined more clearly by the views of families and children).*
- *Integrated front-line delivery (breaking down the existing organisational and cultural barriers of different service providers such as schools and police).*
- *Integrated processes (getting help to children more efficiently and quickly).*
- *Integrated strategy (pooling funding and resources).*
- *Inter-agency governance (clear frameworks for collective strategic planning, resource allocation and accountabilities).*

(DCSF, 2008b, p1)

In 2007 the government reviewed the effectiveness of trusts and issued further guidance to help them improve inter-agency co-operation as part of *The Children's Plan: Building brighter futures* (DCSF, 2008a), which includes government goal-setting for provision for children by 2020. It will be discussed again in Chapter 12.

What is clear is that the problems associated with the bringing together of distinct professions with separate remits, such as schools and social services, are profound ones. Each agency has its own legislative duties and is funded and accountable for its actions through separate and highly rigorous target-setting and assessment. In school, for example, we have a statutory duty to deliver the National Curriculum and raise standards in core subjects. Income is based on numbers in school and separate target-driven funding for key central government initiatives, such as improving level scores in literacy and numeracy. Schools, heads and teachers are assessed and frequently financially rewarded through performance-related pay based on statistical improvements in pupil performance in literacy and numeracy, or the GCSE A–C achievement (George and Clay, 2008). Alternatively, social services have a statutory duty to safeguard children and to work with parents to prevent abuse or neglect. They work individually on a case-by-case basis and are judged predominantly by their failures and their ability to manage extensive workloads. They have limited budgets. Traditionally, they have worked for the welfare of the family, not for that of individual children. Their interest in the education of children is inevitably limited. Safety is their first concern (Parton, 2006; Appleton and Stanley, 2008).

As is obvious, these two agents for children's well-being are quite different. Add the police to the mix, with their duty to protect the public and catch criminals measured by their achievement of government-determined targets for convictions and crime reduction, and we can see that natural co-operation and sharing might be challenging in the extreme. Working together and sharing funding may appear to be unworkable. It is unsurprising that the government is having to consider making legislative changes to help overcome this professional isolationism, born not of lack of willingness, but of rigidity of rules, protocols and accountability and funding issues.

The Children's Commissioner

The Children's Commissioner for England was first appointed in March 2005. His role was to give voice to children and young people and act as an advocate for their rights at the highest level of government. He has a particular remit to represent the voice of the most vulnerable in society. Independent from government, the Commissioner is able to challenge policy and practice at all levels. Sir Al Aynsley-Green, the current Commisioner, has already spoken out publicly about the negative impact of school testing on the well-being of children. While he stopped short of calling for an end to national testing, he was nevertheless highly critical of the testing of young children (Bawden, 2007, pp8–9). You might like to visit the Commissioner's website at **www.childrenscommissioner.org.uk** to see what his views and actions are.

Sharing information: the Common Assessment Framework

Inter-agency collaboration, including multi-agency teams, aims now to work in one geographical place, often in schools, with a lead professional for each child acting as co-ordinator and advocate for each individual child (Dagley et al., 2008). To facilitate communication, the Common Assessment Framework (CAF) (September 2008) is the latest reform to be introduced. It is a common national database of information for all agencies, so that any information from the police, social services, medical and health services and education is automatically recorded in one file under the name of the child. In schools, the named person given the responsibility for accessing and entering information is frequently the Special Educational Needs Co-ordinator (SENCO), but it may well be that highly qualified teaching assistants (level 4 grade) may be given this responsibility. To investigate further some of the critical perspectives on CAF, read Gilligan and Manby (2008).

> ### REFLECTIVE TASK
> Stop for a moment and think, first, about the advantages of this unified electronic database. Then consider the dangers and disadvantages. What would be needed to overcome these difficulties? Talk to your proposed CAF officer in your educational setting. What do they think about this issue of advantage and disadvantage and the safeguards needed?

The ECM's impact on education provision

The CAF is not the only thing to impact on education provision, though it might be the most important at the moment. Take time now to consider the five outcomes of the ECM. Use a diagram, such as the one below, to record your ideas and where your educational setting delivers or meets these aims. Is it in something they teach (the curriculum), something they do (procedures, rules, routines), something they provide outside teaching the curriculum (support, opportunities for extra-curricular activities, playground games and apparatus) or the way they treat one another and others, such as families and other agencies? What is valued by the leaders and staff (ethos, mission, behaviour management, priorities, partnership in practice, communication)?

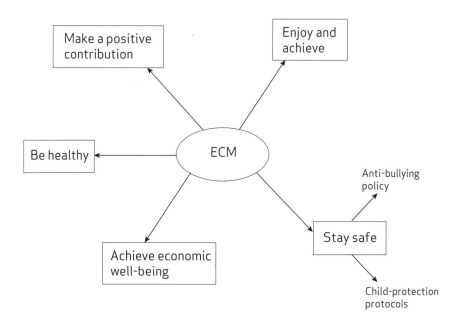

The curriculum

The ECM agenda enshrined in the Children Act 2004 made a noticeable difference to schools in terms of their curriculum provision. Along with the Ofsted-prompted DfES (2003b) *Excellence and Enjoyment* requirements, there was suddenly a mandatory demand for the school's curriculum to become more holistic, or suited to education of the whole child, not just their academic brains. This meant that subjects such as art and craft, design technology, music, PE and the humanities of history, geography and RE became more significant, though core National Tests still dominate subject priorities in schools. This issue will be addressed in greater detail in Chapter 10. It became important to enable children and young people to develop skills and talents in all areas, even if some of that came about through extra-curricular study or the opportunities created by the white paper *14–19 Education and Skills* (DCSF, 2005), with its alternative options for apprenticeship and further education courses. This is discussed further in Chapter 11.

Enjoy and achieve

The requirement that children should 'enjoy' their study had all the appearances of being a revolutionary idea, though seasoned teachers will recall the pre-back-to-basics era of education (before 1993) during which, at least in primary settings, fun and enjoyment in class were normal ways of learning. It was seen in secondary schools also, before the Education Reform Act 1988, when teachers provided extra-curricular clubs and activities out of goodwill. Issues revolving around the motivation of pupils have finally been acknowledged by central government as a key factor in achievement levels (DfES, 2004). Motivation, including the excitement and pleasure of learning, remains a central focus for support staff and learning mentors, since frequently it is this group of professionals who are obliged to re-motivate the disaffected towards learning. One may wish to ask why there is a need for re-motivation if the system is so good.

> **PRACTICAL TASK**
> We know that outside factors, such as an anarchic upbringing or poverty, influence the motivation of pupils in school but, for now, spend a few minutes asking yourself what the education system itself does to pupils to turn them off learning. Consider how these demotivating effects could be challenged and changed. Write down your ideas and share them with your colleagues or fellow students. See if you can change at least one thing that might demotivate pupils.

Make a positive contribution

Inevitably, one wonders if the government considered this outcome to revolve around economic productivity, but a more global interpretation is taken in schools with the emphasis on active citizenship and voluntary action for charity. Economic productivity is seen as a direct result of raised standards of achievement in schools, particularly in the realm of global competition, as our government is so fond of reminding us. We are seeing a revival of the teaching of money management skills and business enterprise skills, piloted in the 1980s. Most schools at primary and secondary level have always incorporated voluntary work or collections and events to raise money for charitable causes. Citizenship, however, was only introduced into the formal curriculum in 2002, when it became mandatory in secondary school settings. It was ECM that led to its introduction in primary school settings, with its attached practices of schools' councils and promoting pupil voice. There are links also to the Children's Rights agenda, promoted by UNICEF and forming the central core of school missions and behaviour management in some schools. For more information on this visit the UNICEF website at **www.unicef.org.uk/tz/resources/download.asp**.

Achieve economic well-being

This outcome brought a sharp emphasis on the value of a taught personal, social and health education (PSHE) curriculum, a subject that emerged in the 1980s but became largely dead and gone during the 1990s and early twenty-first century. Most schools at primary and secondary level now have dedicated curriculum time for this aspect of learning. Social and emotional aspects of learning (SEAL) programmes were introduced in 2004 at primary level as a direct result of the ECM agenda and of a recognition that behaviour and achievement were influenced by personal and social well-being or a lack of it (DfES, 2004; Jones, 2006; Weare, 2007; Crow, 2008). SEAL units are now being introduced at Key Stage 3 and are likely to be the province of support staff and Higher Level Teaching Assistant (HLTA) status holders to pilot and deliver, as they frequently are at primary level.

This outcome also demanded that schools look again at their ethos and climate, what they provide for pupils when not in the class and how they incorporate pupil voice in the management and functioning of the school. Has your educational setting recently revised its mission statement or considered ethos as part of its school improvement plan?

PRACTICAL TASK

You might like to look up your school's mission statement and see how far it reflects the language and aims of the ECM agenda. As always, I also urge you to make an honest appraisal of whether what is written is mirrored in actual day-to-day practice. Where it is not, try to work out why that is so and how the problem could be tackled.

Be healthy

The separate outcome of being healthy meant that health education had to be strengthened with the help of the revised Healthy Schools Status (DfES, 2005). It didn't stop with the development of health education programmes, however. The Healthy Schools Awards demanded that policies and practice for healthy eating in snack provision and school meals be followed, regular exercise became important and hygiene was addressed. Drugs and sex education policies and curricula were introduced or revised.

REFLECTIVE TASK

Identify your school's provision of services, amenities and curriculum to promote healthy lifestyles. How effective is it? How does this provision impact on your personal practice? Are you living a more healthy lifestyle because of your job and place of work? Spend some time thinking about what limits the effectiveness of what the school does for its pupils or for its staff to promote a healthy lifestyle. How can these constraints be eliminated or counteracted?

Stay safe

Perhaps it is this aspect of the ECM agenda that will show the most change in school practice, for safeguarding children now requires schools to be far more collaborative and proactive. This is where we will see school staff forming part of multi-disciplinary teams to monitor the daily safety of vulnerable pupils or pupils at risk. Of course, this always happened for pupils with statements of special needs, where multiple professionals were involved in reviews of progress, and has also existed where children have been placed on the 'at risk' register, or where children are victims of abuse. Now the term 'vulnerable children' is being interpreted much more broadly and includes pupils in danger of exclusion and who truant, pupils who are carers, pupils who are emotionally vulnerable, including those with diagnosed mental health conditions, and pupils who have generated concern from any of the children's service providers. There will be the appointment of named lead professionals or key workers who have responsibility to co-ordinate the multi-agency information and liaise with the pupil and their guardians. They will also act in an advocacy role for the pupil. Meetings of the team are most likely to happen in school and you may already be seeing the building or colonisation of space by representatives of other children's services, social workers, police, health professionals and the CAMHS (Child and Adolescent Mental Health Service). You might be part of that team as someone who best knows the pupil and his or her learning and life. In time, we may see highly skilled support staff taking those lead professional roles.

The 'stay safe' outcome also extends to the prevention and addressing of bullying issues. The first report of the Children's Society's international *Good Childhood* survey (2006) identified that British children feel very unsafe at school and that bullying is one of their greater fears and threats. The SEAL materials have bullying as one of their seven annual themes. Schools must have a policy in place to prevent it and deal with it quickly and fairly and this must be acted upon in practice.

PRACTICAL TASK

Seek out your setting's anti-bullying policy, then talk to the head teacher and the lunchtime welfare staff about how this is implemented in practice. Talk to some pupils about what they think bullying is and how it can be prevented, or how it should be dealt with. It will be an interesting conversation.

It seems that 'staying safe' may be one of the hardest and most urgent outcomes of this agenda. As yet we do not appear to have ensured in any way that all pupils can be safe in schools.

The role of the teaching assistant in ECM implementation

We've already discussed some of the ways in which support staff are integral to the implementation of the ECM agenda. The following case studies illustrate this in day-to-day ways. Read them and identify where the ECM agenda is being fulfilled.

Case Study 1

Suzie is a full-time level 4 learning mentor in a primary school in an area of extreme social deprivation where there is a prevailing culture of unemployment. The school takes most of the pupils previously excluded from the other schools in the area, thus the school has a very high number of children statemented for emotional, social and behavioural difficulties. There is a low achievement rate for National Tests and a problem with attendance. Despite this, the staff are highly committed to their role in raising aspirations and the environment is one characterised by its calmness, colourful displays and care.

Suzie's role is multifarious. She begins her day at 8.20 a.m. by calling at the homes of five pupils who struggle to attend and encouraging them to come with her to school. When she arrives with her pupils she goes into a staff briefing, which includes her valuable update on the well-being of her five reluctant pupils. While morning assembly is going on she has a meeting with 12 pupils for whom she has special responsibility. She celebrates the successes of the day before, reminds them of their learning and behaviour targets and encourages them to 'keep cool and tuned in'. She gives them the times in the day when she will be withdrawing them from class to work on the social and emotional skills in her own classroom area. Throughout the meeting the children eat as much hot toast as they want and drink orange juice. They finish with a group hug and a rallying cry of 'we're great, we can do it!'

After classes begin, she takes her groups for SEAL-inspired games and activities that conclude with a calming story and soft music. During break time she goes out on to the playground and watches her pupils. Frequently she is involved in helping the pupils negotiate conflict and defuse aggression. The teachers really value her for this intermediary role.

Her sessions continue in the late morning, then at lunchtime she spends the time offering a drop-in chat session. This is open to all pupils, not just those for whom she has special responsibility.

In the afternoon she is involved in supporting a pupil who has lost his temper and thrown a chair at a teacher. He's run off, but soon returns to school. She talks to him, calming him down and then going with him to the head teacher, where he is temporarily excluded. As his lone parent is not available, Suzie keeps him with her until the end of the day, when she walks him back to his home and talks to his dad about the incident.

Finally she goes home, having made notes on the encounter. Tomorrow is another day.

REFLECTIVE TASK

Looking at case study 1, what aspects of the ECM agenda is Suzie fulfilling in her role? What benefits to the school and the pupils does she bring?

CASE STUDY 2

Martin is a full-time level 2 learning support assistant in an urban high school, having formally been a science technician in the same school. He spends his day supporting Sam, a Year 8 boy, with a statement for autistic spectrum disorder. He accompanies the boy to his classes and then works one to one with him to help him cope with the pace and variation of the lessons. He adapts resources when he's given the chance, though mostly he has to do this 'on the hoof' as teachers hand out worksheets. The boy enjoys maths and science and behaves well in these sessions. His achievement in these areas in good, but in English he becomes frustrated and doesn't understand inferences and demands for aesthetic appreciation of the text. Although he can read, he has times when he refuses to take part and can become aggressive and withdrawn. Sometimes Martin is allowed to withdraw Sam from the English class and teach him one to one. The school considers this anti-inclusionary, but the English teacher finds it a relief when permission is given for Martin to withdraw Sam.

Martin accompanies Sam on his breaks, though he tries to keep in the background to avoid making Sam dependent upon him socially. What he does do is watch for signs that Sam is being taunted, made fun of or wound up deliberately by other pupils. Twice he has intervened on Sam's behalf when he was being bullied. Martin reported the incidents and the school acted to stop that behaviour. Martin considers that the other pupils tolerate Sam because he doesn't want to interfere in their groups or sports, but he also believes Sam may be lonely. He has plans to begin an after-school science club, which he thinks would bring Sam into contact with other science enthusiasts. He spends the end of his day talking to Sam's mum over the phone (Sam is taxied home), briefing her about Sam's day. Once a term, Martin gives a report to the SENCO on Sam's progress with his targets and attends the Individual Education Plan (IEP) review meeting with Sam.

REFLECTIVE TASK

- Looking at case study 2, in what ways is Martin enabling the school to meet its ECM outcomes? What benefits is he bringing to the school?
- How could his role be adapted to make it more effective in meeting the ECM outcomes?

CASE STUDY 3

Jamie is a part-time level 1 teaching assistant in a primary school. She works in the Year 4 class under the supervision and direction of the class teacher. She photocopies, helps with displays and helps get out and put away resources. Her main work during class time is to support groups of children with their numeracy and literacy work. She is given an activity plan by the teacher that tells her what the objective for the group is and what to do. She usually works with the children who struggle with maths and English. Jamie really enjoys this work and wants to get her NVQ Level 2 qualification so she can achieve promotion and do more work with pupils. She enjoys helping the children understand the point of what they are doing and she tries to ensure that the activities are made more fun, though she is conscious that she must keep the noise down.

The children seem to relish working with her. Sometimes they talk to her about their home lives or when they are worried about something. Jamie listens sympathetically and once or twice has felt obliged to pass on the information she has been given to the teacher, having told the pupil she would need to do this. She worries a bit about a couple of pupils who seem unloved and unhappy. She brought in some of her children's old PE kit so that, if these pupils forget their kit, she can lend it to them. She wishes she could do more but it wouldn't be right. It would be interfering and offensive to the parents and unfair to the other pupils in the class.

REFLECTIVE TASK

- Looking at case study 3, on the surface you might assume that Jamie is actually not involved much in the ECM agenda, and that she is more used to delivering National Curriculum objectives, but can you find where she might be contributing to the ECM outcomes?
- Is Jamie right in her final thoughts? There is no right or wrong answer here, but think through the advantages of intervention and the problems that might occur if she did interfere.

PRACTICAL TASK

Now it's your turn. Using the diagram you used for identifying the school's delivery of ECM (see page 7), place yourself in the centre and identify how you contribute to meeting the outcomes of the ECM agenda.

Constraints on ECM implementation

The ECM agenda has the potential to make a real and positive impact on childhood well-being. Its roll-out, however, has already faced difficulties and the outcomes are likely to be undermined by conflicting demands, priorities and policies (Hudson, 2006). Multi-agency integration has yet to be resolved, though the government seems resolved to push it through. It will need to be pushed, because there are fundamental and entrenched differences in purpose, procedures and culture in each of the participating professions.

Time in school is another precious commodity: time and staff. Looking after the whole child takes resources and inevitably those are rationed. Perhaps the greatest constraint on its full implementation is the lack of commitment within society to actually pay for and prioritise children's well-being through taxation (Roche and Tucker, 2007). There may be a prevailing attitude in this country that the welfare of children is a parental responsibility, something also fully recognised by the government, and it is inappropriate for the state to interfere in that. The words 'nanny state' are frequently cited in the populist press when issues of state-sponsored intervention in the lives of parents and families arise. Some of society's views also seditiously imply that making a fuss of children and over-protecting them might actually do more harm than good. The children will be spoilt and helpless if they don't learn to overcome difficulties and get on with life. This is a more difficult constraint to overcome, because it is, in part, valid. There have been recently articulated concerns over excessive health and safety restrictions in children's play areas and fear of paedophilial-driven child kidnapping and murder. Certainly, in the BBC documentary *A Child of Our Time* (2008), their surveys of children and their parents identify severe restrictions in independent movement and imaginative and creative play, often replaced with supervised and physically safe play, car transport and organised activities. The children interviewed expressed a nebulous but powerful fear of being 'out there without an adult'; 'It's dangerous, I might get hurt.' Sue Palmer's book, *Toxic Childhood* (2006), also highlights this issue as one of many impacting upon the happiness and health of children.

You will already have witnessed, in any educational setting, inequalities in the life chances of pupils and it is important to recall that there are some children for whom state intervention in the name of the ECM aims to make a difference, quite literally, between life and death. One simply has to remember the original impetus for this legislation to understand its importance.

The future of ECM

There is more reform to come. The integration of services and genuine multi-disciplinary teamwork led by key workers or lead professionals supported by a common information database have yet to be realised. Children's Trusts have yet to be refined and to function effectively. At a school level we are already seeing the employment of more learning mentors, counsellors, pastoral support leaders and nurture group managers. Home–school liaison is being developed, with the appointment of outreach workers. There is a move towards alternative curricula, such as that practised in nurture groups and further education and work-based settings. There is even a trend towards educating away from conventional schools for a whole range of children's groups. Children's centres are engaging in education for whole families, including children. We are seeing the development of a national pay and grading for those in the children's workforce, with extended and nationally recognised academic and vocational qualifications, such as the Early Years Professional Status and Foundation degrees, to improve the knowledge and skills base of those directly involved in the support of children. Of most interest will be the pressures of accountability that impose priorities in schools. One wonders how long it will take for the outcomes of the ECM agenda to overtake achievement in National Tests as a measure of school effectiveness. Perhaps that will be never. What is your view?

CHAPTER SUMMARY

- The ECM agenda is an ongoing process of central government reform of all services that come into contact with children.
- Its first aims were enshrined in the Children Act 2004 and subsequent legislation related to health provision, youth justice and local government has also driven forward the aims of the agenda.
- Schools must now take account of ECM's five outcomes in their work, processes and procedures.
- There has been increased pastoral support built into the education provision and many schools now have multi-agency teams working from their sites.
- We may be seeing a shift in attitudes towards children where their rights and needs are geninely prioritised. The impact of this long-term reform, however, will not be able to be fully assessed until many years from now.
- These reforms might still be reversed and discarded by subsequent governments or ECM might stall and become tokenistic because of professional demarcation and lack of commitment.

- Support staff, like other child-centred professionals, will continue to be committed to meeting children's needs and reducing inequalities for the deprived.
- In the end, it isn't legislation that brings about change; it's the heart and will of the personnel that make a difference.

REFERENCES

Appleton, J. and Stanley, N. (2008) Safeguarding children – everyone's responsibility. *Child Abuse Review*, 17(1): 1–5.

Bawden, A. (2007) Walking back to happiness. *Guardian*, 20 March: 8–9.

Children's Society (2006) *Good Childhood Enquiry: The launch report*. Available online at www.childrenssociety.org.uk (accessed 15 January 2009).

Crow, F. (2008) Learning for well-being: personal, social and health education and a changing curriculum. *Pastoral Care in Education*, 26(1): 43–52.

Dagley, V., Howe, A., Salter, C., Brandon, M., Warren, C. and Black, J. (2007) Implications of the New Common Assessment Framework and lead professional working for pastoral care staff in schools. *Pastoral Care in Education*, 25(1): 4–10.

Department for Children, Schools and Families (DCSF) (2005) *14–19 Education and Skills* (white paper). London: TSO.

Department for Children, Schools and Families (DCSF) (2008a) *The Children's Plan: Building brighter futures*. London: TSO.

Department for Children, Schools and Families (DCSF) (2008b) *Every Child Matters: Change for children*. Available online at www. everychildmatters.gov.uk/ (accessed 18 August 2008).

Department for Education and Skills (DfES) (2003a) *Every Child Matters*. London: TSO.

Department for Education and Skills (DfES) (2003b) *Excellence and Enjoyment: A strategy for primary schools*. London: TSO.

Department for Education and Skills (DfES) (2004) *Excellence and Enjoyment: Social and emotional aspects of learning*. London: TSO.

George, R. and Clay, J. (2008) Reforming teachers and uncompromising standards: implications for social justice in schools. *Forum For Promoting 3–13 Comprehensive Education*, 50(1): 103–12.

Gilligan, P. and Manby, M. (2008) The Common Assessment Framework: does reality match the rhetoric? *Child and Family Social Work*, 13(2): 177–87.

HM Government (2004) *The Children Act*. London: TSO.

Hudson, B. (2006) User outcomes and children's services reform: ambiguity and conflict in the policy process. *Social Policy and Society*, 5(2): 227–36.

Jones, P. (2006) Status of pastoral care in schools in the 21st century. *Pastoral Care in Education*, 24(2): 64–5.

Palmer, S. (2006) *Toxic Childhood*. London: Orion.

Parton, N. (2006) *Every Child Matters*? The shift to prevention whilst strengthening protection in children's services in England. *Children and Youth Services Review*, 28(8): 976–91.

Roche, J. and Tucker, S. (2007) *Every Child Matters*: 'tinkering' or 'reforming'? – an analysis of the development of the Children Act (2004) from an educational perspective. *Education Three to Thirteen*, 35(3): 213–24.

Weare, C. (2007) Delivering *Every Child Matters*: the central role of social and emotional learning in schools. *Education Three to Thirteen*, 35(3): 239–48.

FURTHER READING

Adams, P. (2007) Learning and caring in the age of the five outcomes. *Education Three to Thirteen*, 35(3): 225–38.

Adams, P. and Tucker, S. (2007) *Every Child Matters*: change for children in schools. *Education Three to Thirteen*, 35(3): 209–12.

Aynsley-Green, A. (2004) Is all well with children and childhood and the health-related services provided for them in contemporary society? Exploiting the opportunities for change. *Paediatrics and Child Health*, 14(3): 237–45.

Best, R. (2007) The whole child matters: the challenge of *Every Child Matters* for pastoral care. *Education Three to Thirteen*, 35(3): 249–60.

Chand, A. (2008) Every Child Matters? A critical review of child welfare reforms in the context of ethnic minority children and families. *Child Abuse Review*, 17(1): 6–22.

Groom, B. (2006) Building relationships for learning: the developing role of the teaching assistant. *Support for Learning*, 21(4): 199–203.

Harris, B. (2006) *Every Child Matters*: A new dawn for pastoral care? *Pastoral Care in Education*, 24(2): 2–4.

Harris, B. (2006) Overview of *Every Child Matters* (2003) and the Children Act (2004). *Pastoral Care in Education*, 24(2) : 5–6.

Harris, B., Vincent, K., Thomson, P. and Toalster, R. (2006) Does every child know they matter? Pupils' views of one alternative to exclusion. *Pastoral Care in Education*, 24(2): 28–38.

Lewis, J. (2006) The school's role in encouraging behaviour for learning outside the classroom that supports learning within. A response to the *Every Child Matters* and *Extended Schools* initiatives. *Support for Learning*, 21(4): 175–81.

Marshall, H. (2006) Professionalism and whole primary school factors aiding and impeding the work of the Learning Mentor. *Support for Learning*, 21(4): 194–8.

Parton, N. (2008) The 'Change for Children' programme in England: towards the 'Preventative-Surveillance State'. *Journal of Law and Society*, 35(1): 166–71.

Soan, S. (2006) Are the needs of children and young people with social, emotional and behavioural needs being served within a multi-agency framework? *Support for Learning*, 21(4): 210–15.

Stern, J. (2007) Mattering: what it means to matter in school. *Education Three to Thirteen*, 35(3): 283–94.

2 SUPPORT STAFF AS PROFESSIONALS

Anita Walton

CHAPTER OBJECTIVES

By the end of this chapter you will:

- know how the teaching assistant profession has changed;
- understand what is meant by being a professional;
- be able to reflect on the real challenges and dilemmas of professionalism within the workplace.

LINKS TO **HLTA** STANDARDS

1. Have high expectations of children and young people with a commitment to helping them fulfil their potential.

2. Establish fair, respectful, trusting, supportive and constructive relationships with children and young people.

3. Demonstrate the positive values, attitudes and behaviour they expect from children and young people.

4. Communicate effectively and sensitively with children, young people, colleagues, parents and carers.

5. Recognise and respect the contribution that parents and carers can make to the development and well-being of children and young people.

6. Demonstrate a commitment to collaborative and co-operative working with colleagues.

7. Improve their own knowledge and practice, including responding to advice and feedback.

Introduction

This chapter will look at how the teaching assistant (TA) role as a professional has grown and developed over the last few years. It will give you time to reflect on what is meant by being a professional in a work context and it will explore some of the challenges and dilemmas that can face you when working with a team of professionals and with children and parents.

The development of the profession

If you have been working within the school environment for a while, take a few minutes to think about how things have changed in relation to the work and role of TAs. If you are relatively new to this role you might like to ask more experienced colleagues about this.

In recent years there has been an increasing number of TAs in both primary and secondary schools.

- There was a 97 per cent increase in the number of support staff between 1997 and 2005, from 136,500 to 268,600.
- This compares with only an 8 per cent increase in the number of teachers over the same period.
- DfES figures suggest one of the fastest-growing groups over this period is TAs, with numbers rising from 61,300 to 148,500 (TDA, 2006).

There has also been a change in role and responsibilities. These changes are partly a result of education reform in the 1980s, which followed the Warnock Report of 1978, when the number of TAs was increased specifically to work with pupils with special educational needs.

There was a growing concern in the late 1990s that a number of reforms had increased the workload and accountability of teachers. The Department for Education and Skills (DfES) commissioned PriceWaterhouseCoopers (2001) to undertake an investigation into teacher workload, which led to a policy to remodel the workforce (DfES, 2003b). According to Mansaray (2006, p172):

> *The authors of the report recommended more innovative deployment of support staff to take over administrative tasks. TAs would be encouraged to take on greater teaching roles, allowing teachers guaranteed non-contact time for planning, preparation and assessment (PPA) and reduced workloads.*

In 2001, Estelle Morris, who was then Secretary of State for Education, announced at a speech to the Social Market Foundation that:

> *Teaching assistants will be*
> - *supervising classes that are undertaking work set by a teacher, or working with small groups of pupils on reading practice;*
> - *supervising lunchtime activities and invigilating tests;*
> - *giving pastoral and other individual support to pupils, and covering for teacher absence;*

- *spending more of their time on teaching, lesson preparation, assessing individual pupil progress and updating their professional skills.*

(Morris, 2001, p16)

Workforce reform, following the Workforce Agreement (DfES, 2003b) meant that duties previously carried out by teachers would be passed on to support staff. These duties included planning and taking whole classes. The Higher Level Teaching Assistant (HLTA) status was introduced in which teaching assistants were assessed against standards very similar to those of the Qualified Teacher status (DfES/TTA, 2003). These policies and developing practices led towards a professionalisation of teaching assistants; however, TAs in general had few professional development opportunities that allowed them to acquire reflective strategies (Lee, 2002). Continuing professional development (CPD) tended to be focused on teachers rather than TAs. Potter and Richardson agreed with this view, and commented that, while teachers are expected to evaluate their own practice, little attention had been given to the needs of classroom assistants to develop critical reflection skills:

Given the increasingly educational role of classroom assistants in both mainstream and special schools, there is a need to ensure that they become reflective practitioners within classroom teams.

(1999, p36)

In 2004 the remit of the Training and Development Agency (TDA) for schools was enhanced to include responsibility for the training and development of the wider school workforce, so that the whole school team could work together for standards to be raised (TDA, 2005). In 2006 the TDA published a three-year strategy for support staff training and development. TAs are now aware that there is an emphasis on training and professional development for them so that their role can be developed even further. The strategy has three main objectives.

1. *Support schools as they develop new ways of training and deploying their support staff.*
2. *Create a framework of standards and qualifications to enable schools to develop the potential of all support staff.*
3. *Extend training opportunities to meet the development needs of all support staff.*

(TDA, 2006, p9)

According to the TDA, support staff are at the heart of school reform, particularly with the emergence of new HLTA and specialist roles. The emergence and implementation of the *Every Child Matters* agenda (DFES, 2003a) has also led to the radical development of pastoral roles for TAs. They will require confidence in their ability and the possibility to develop and achieve a more professional status. The TDA advocates that performance development systems should be developed for all staff, so that the whole school workforce can concentrate on improving practice and personal development.

PRACTICAL TASK

Do you or your colleagues have a system of work appraisal in your workplace? Find out more about this.

What is meant by 'professional'?

The term 'professional' crops up in many phrases and has a variety of meanings. Phrases used include: 'being a professional', 'education professional', 'professional development' and 'behaving professionally'.

REFLECTIVE TASK
What do you think is meant by the term 'professional?' List the key words and phrases that you come up with.

Characteristics of being professional

Respect

Being professional involves being respectful to all staff, pupils, parents and colleagues. Professionals should foster an atmosphere of mutual respect. Your behaviour to pupils should be such that the pupil understands that they are respected and valued. You can do this by:

- communicating in a way that they will be able to understand, which may be different for varying age groups and pupils who have difficulties in communicating;
- being fair and inclusive;
- using positive language;
- supporting pupils to show respect in their communication with each other.

REFLECTIVE TASK
In what other ways can you show pupils that you respect and value them?

Confidentiality

As a professional, you will also need to respect the confidentiality of information relating to pupils. You may have seen information on Individual Education Plans (IEPs) and marks and levels relating to their work.

You may have access to, or knowledge of, sensitive information about pupils and it is imperative that this information remains confidential. Sometimes you would not even share this information with colleagues if they have no reason to be aware of it. Always check before divulging any information about a pupil to colleagues and take great care that you always respect confidentiality. You may divulge something inadvertently during a casual conversation or you may think that someone already knows, so always be vigilant.

CASE STUDY 1

Josie Springer works at Rosemary Street Primary School as a TA. Last Saturday, in the supermarket, one of her pupils' parents approached her and asked how she thought Stephen was doing in his reading. Josie replied 'He is on level 6 and doing really well; he's one of the best readers in the class, and has even overtaken George.' On Monday, George's father demanded to speak to the class teacher and complained that confidential information about his son's reading level was given to a parent.

In this case study, Josie did act unprofessionally as she should not have discussed another pupil's work or level with Stephen's parents. This case study shows how difficult it is to know what to say when approached in an informal setting. Clearly, Josie did not have access to pupil records at the supermarket, and should she have said anything without discussing it with the teacher?

REFLECTIVE TASK

In case study 1, how do you think Josie should have responded to Stephen's parent?

CASE STUDY 2

Peter is a special needs support assistant who works with a Year 5 boy called Danny, who has emotional and behavioural difficulties. Peter has formed a very close relationship with Danny and his family. Prior to a review meeting, Peter read a very negative report about Danny's progress written by the SENCO. It concluded with a strong recommendation for removal to a special school. Concerned that Danny's parents would be taken by surprise at the review meeting by this report, he photocopied it and sent it anonymously to the parents.

In this case study Peter acted unprofessionally. His concern for Danny's parents was no excuse for him divulging this information.

REFLECTIVE TASK

Looking at case study 2, what do you think are the potential consequences of Peter's actions for Peter, the school and for Danny?

Professional conduct and behaviour in school

Respecting colleagues

Being a professional in school involves conducting yourself in a professional manner. This involves working collaboratively with colleagues and respecting their professional expertise. Sometimes it will be a specialist who you will have to work with, such as a social worker or a speech and language therapist, rather than a teacher and you will need to make sure that you understand and follow any instructions. If you are not sure what you are meant to do, ask them to explain it to you.

Part of being a professional means having a professional approach at all times and being careful about all conversations you have when in earshot of the pupils.

CASE STUDY 3

Two TAs, Jane and Stephen, were in a study support area where pupils were engaged in independent research. Jane said to Stephen 'I'm not looking forward to the next class, I've got Mrs Taylor doing history and she hasn't got a clue about the kids and her lessons are always boring.'

Sometimes professionals working in schools make judgements about other professionals in a casual conversation. This could be viewed as being unprofessional. In this case study, Jane was clearly acting unprofessionally as she could be heard by the pupils. Instead, she should have thought about her role in the lesson and how she could work with the teacher to have a positive impact on the lesson.

REFLECTIVE TASK
Looking at case study 3, how would you respond if you were Stephen?

Voicing concerns

Most of the time teachers and TAs are clear about their roles in the classroom. In the real world, however, TAs may be asked to undertake work they do not feel confident about. In these circumstances you must voice your concerns and ask for advice. State clearly exactly what it is that you are concerned about and why. Voicing your concerns does not mean that you are being unprofessional. Being part of a professional team means that you are able to discuss situations and problems that are difficult for you.

CASE STUDY 4

Susan is a secondary school general TA working across all departments. The head of the ICT department had set up a lesson in the ICT room involving researching on the internet for a personal project with Year 8. Susan was assisting the ICT teacher who, halfway through the lesson, told her that he was feeling ill, and could she monitor the class and dismiss them at the end of the lesson. Susan is a relatively new TA employed at level 2 and she didn't feel she could take this class, but was frightened of getting into trouble, so she agreed. Towards the end of the lesson she noticed that some of the class had managed to access an internet chat room and were giggling and posting messages. She asked them to close down the site and return to their work, but they refused.

In this case study, Susan should have told the teacher that she didn't feel confident to take the class on her own and asked if she could send one of the pupils to the office so that someone could be sent to cover the lesson. Sometimes not voicing concerns earlier enough can cause more problems later on.

Dress code

According to research by Fortenberry et al. (1978), Forsythe et al. (1984) and Kim and Lennon (2005), the clothes we wear can have a significant influence on how we are perceived by others. Dress can convey personal characteristics, such as decisiveness and authoritativeness. Dressing smartly suggests that we respect our position as a professional.

Most schools would expect:

- clothing to be clean;
- clothing to not be shabby;
- clothing to be properly fitting;
- clothing to not look sloppy;
- clothing to be appropriate for the setting;
- clothing to not have slogans or represent a particular following.

Take a few minutes to think about why dressing in a certain way matters. What messages are received by children, young people, parents and other professionals when we dress professionally? Ask your colleagues what they think would be professional dress. Do they think the type of clothes you wear in school is important in the way you are perceived by staff, pupils and parents?

Timekeeping

I have always been a quarter of an hour before my time, and it has made a man of me.

Lord Nelson

TAs need to provide good models of behaviour to pupils by organising and managing their activities responsibly and effectively while practising good timekeeping. Punctuality does not just apply to first thing in the morning when you arrive at school. It applies after breaks and lunch, and being punctual for each lesson. It is very disrespectful to be late without a good reason, and your late arrival in the classroom could interrupt others while they are talking.

It can, however, be very difficult to arrive in plenty of time to undertake your work, particularly if you have to move from one side of the building to the other.

PRACTICAL TASK
Consider your own timekeeping. Are there any ways you could improve this? Make a list of recommendations for yourself and try them out, and discuss stress points with the key professionals concerned.

Language and non-verbal communication

As professionals, TAs will be expected to communicate using acceptable language. Unacceptable language would include:

- swearing;
- negative language;

- language that is disrespectful;
- inappropriate language of a sexual nature;
- language that is racist, sexist or disrespectful to a religion.

Discuss with colleagues what is and is not acceptable language to use in your work environment. Is there a difference between communicating with staff and with children or young people? Explore why codes of language are important to professionalism.

We communicate to others through body language as well as words. In some ways this posturing is more powerful than speech. According to Mehrabian (1971) there are three elements to communication: spoken words, tone of voice and body language. In his research he determined the following generalisations.

- 7 per cent of communication happens in spoken words.
- 38 per cent of communication happens through voice tone.
- 55 per cent of communication happens via general body language.

CASE STUDY 5

Paul is a Year 7 pupil who wanted to get his bag out of his form room at lunchtime as his lunch was in it. David, a Year 11 pupil, stood in front of the classroom door so that Paul couldn't get in. Paul asked to go into the classroom. David crossed his arms, stared at the pupil for about ten seconds, and then said 'I don't think so.' Paul asked again if he could go into the classroom, but David just shrugged his shoulders and stared at him again. Paul looked upset and walked away without his lunch.

In this case study, David, by staring, was conveying an aggressive attitude and crossing his arms showed that he wasn't going to move. Shrugging his shoulders conveyed that he didn't care about what Paul wanted.

PRACTICAL TASK

Spend some time now identifying postures that would be considered as being unfriendly, uninterested, bored or frightened. Look out for these in the workplace environment. Pupils may be good sources for this. Think about how negative body language can have an impact on your pupils, your colleagues and other professionals?

Now think about how we can convey interest, enthusiasm, openness, assertiveness and confidence through body language. Practise these in front of a mirror. Become more aware of your body language and start to incorporate positive posturing and stances.

Suggestions for professional conduct in school

- Make sure you are aware of the expected professional code of dress for the school.
- Make sure you are always on time for lessons, duties or meetings.
- Try to be positive in your language and your non-verbal communication.

Involvement in the school

Being a professional also means being involved in whole-school matters and staff meetings. You will also need an awareness of school organisational needs and sensitivity to pupil and staff needs. You may also need subject expertise and skills when working with certain pupils or classes.

As a TA you will be working as a member of a professional team or several professional teams and you will probably be taking on several roles. You will need to know when to use your initiative, when to seek advice, when to speak and when not to. If you are liaising with other professionals outside school, you will need good communication skills and an understanding of your role within that team. In Chapter 3 you will learn more about working in partnership with other professionals.

PRACTICAL TASK

What kind of professional skills and attitudes would be required when working with the following? Copy and complete the table (the first one has been done for you).

WORKING WITH	PROFESSIONAL SKILLS
Parents	We would expect TAs working with parents to respect the confidentiality of all pupils and staff and to be polite at all times. TAs would be required to know when, and to whom, to refer any issues beyond their sphere of competence.
Teachers	
Multi-agency teams	
After-school clubs	
Whole-school staff meetings	
Small-group settings	
Whole-class settings	
An individual child	
School governors	

Challenges

Why is it sometimes difficult to act professionally?

- Sometimes it is difficult if you are dealing with aggression or unfairness from pupils, parents or staff. You may want to retaliate, but that wouldn't help.
- Some TAs may lack confidence to participate in or contribute to meetings.
- Sometimes it is difficult to be positive if you are not feeling very well.

REFLECTIVE TASK

What do you think are the challenges to acting professionally?

HLTA standards for professional values and practice

The list below shows the HLTA standards that are concerned with professional attributes.

Here is an example for the first standard.

Example

I run an after-school club for Year 7 and 8 pupils who are having difficulty in maths lessons. We use maths games on the computer and I try to give lots of individual feedback and praise. The Year 7 and 8 maths teachers have told me that the pupils are now more confident in their maths lessons and are answering questions. At the end of the year, the National Curriculum level has improved in maths for nearly all those who attended the club.

PRACTICAL TASK

First read through these standards and reflect on your own practice. Choose two of the standards and give examples of how you meet each standard.

Professional attributes

Those awarded HLTA status must demonstrate, through their practice, that they:

1. Have high expectations of children and young people with a commitment to helping them fulfil their potential.
   - Demonstrate how you encourage pupils to raise their achievement through increased participation in learning activities.
   - Identify barriers to pupils' participating and achieving and minimise these barriers.
   - Challenge stereotypical views and low expectations of what pupils can achieve.

2. Establish fair, respectful, trusting, supportive and constructive relationships with children and young people.
   - Become familiar with school policies and classroom rules and routines to ensure that pupils are treated in a consistent manner.

- Treat pupils in ways that promote a positive self-image and develop self-esteem and explain reasons for any actions or consequences, taking care not to embarrass them.
- Take an interest in pupils' preferences and attitudes, listen to them and involve them equally in activities.

3. Demonstrate the positive values, attitudes and behaviour they expect from children and young people.
   - Model courteous modes of address and address any name-calling, rudeness or thoughtlessness and inappropriate treatment of property and buildings.
   - Remind pupils of school policies and classroom protocols concerning rights and responsibilities and be familiar with such policies.
   - Deal with subject content that enables promotion of positive values, attitudes and behaviour, e.g. circle time, topic work, PSHE, citizenship, history, literature, educational visits and assembly preparation.
   - Promote a community among groups of pupils from mixed ethnic backgrounds.

4. Communicate effectively and sensitively with children, young people, colleagues, parents and carers.
   - Vary the style of communication depending on the purpose, face-to-face, telephone or written.
   - Be sensitive to variations in family values and practices across and within cultural groupings and avoid assumptions and judgements about parents and carers.
   - Know school policies and procedures.
   - Understand confidentiality requirements, knowing what information to pass on and to whom.
   - Maintain effective boundaries between roles as a member of a community and as a member of school staff.
   - Brief teachers with information about pupils' motivation, behaviour and attainment that teachers can use in reporting to parents.

5. Recognise and respect the contribution that parents and carers can make to the development and well-being of children and young people.
   - Keep parents and carers informed of matters relating to their child.
   - Engage with parents and carers in understanding the needs of the child.
   - Involve parents and carers in children's learning.

6. Demonstrate a commitment to collaborative and co-operative working with colleagues.
   - Demonstrate how your participation in the team contributes to taking forward pupils' learning.
   - Demonstrate that you can take the initiative and make decisions in the context of teachers' guidance and the school's policies and practice.
   - Know when and from whom to seek advice and support.
   - Be aware of issues beyond the scope of your role and refer these to colleagues as appropriate.

7. Improve their own knowledge and practice, including responding to advice and feedback.
   - Demonstrate that you can acquire new knowledge and skills, e.g. training course, e-learning, reading, discussion with colleagues and other professionals.
   - Demonstrate how you acquired new knowledge and then use this to take pupils' learning forward.

- Review and modify your own practice as a result of observation or discussion.
- Demonstrate that you carry out realistic self-evaluation and that you respond to and act upon feedback, e.g. setting targets.
- Improve your own practice on own initiative or through the school CPD arrangements.

(adapted from TDA, 2007)

CHAPTER SUMMARY

- The TA professional has grown and developed over the last few years.
- There are real challenges and dilemmas of professionalism within the workplace.
- You should now be able to reflect on what is meant by being a professional in a work context.

REFERENCES

Department for Education and Skills (DfES) (2003a) *Every Child Matters.* London: TSO.

Department for Education and Skills (DfES (2003b) *Developing the Role of School Support Staff.* London: DFES.

Department for Education and Skills (DfES)/TTA (2003) *Professional Standards for Higher Level Teaching Assistants.* London: DfES/TTA.

Forsythe, S., Drake, M. and Cox, C. (1984) Dress as an influence on the perceptions of management characteristics in women. *Family and Consumer Sciences Research Journal,* 13(2): 112–21.

Fortenberry, J., MacLean, J., Morris, P. and O'Connell, M. (1978) Mode of dress as a perceptual cue to deference. *Journal of Social Psychology,* 104: 139–40.

Kim, M. and Lennon, S. (2005) The effects of customers' dress on salespersons' service in large-sized clothing specialty stores. *Clothing and Textiles Research Journal,* 23(2): 78–87.

Lee, C. (2002) *Teaching Assistants in Schools: The current state of play.* London: NFER.

Mansaray, A. (2006) Liminality and in/exclusion: exploring the work of teaching assistants. *Pedagogy, Culture & Society,* 14: 171–87.

Mehrabian, A. (1971) *Silent messages.* Wadsworth, CA: Belmont.

Morris, E. (2001) *Professionalism and Trust: The future of teachers and teaching.* Available online at www.teachernet.gov.uk/_doc/1042/SMF Report.pdf (accessed 22 October 2007).

PriceWaterhouseCoopers (2001) *Teacher Workload Study. Final Report.* London: DfES.

Potter, C. A. and Richardson, H. L. (1999) Facilitating classroom assistants' professional reflection through video workshops. British Journal of Special Education, 26(1): 34–6.

Training and Development Agency (TDA) (2005) *Building the School Team.* Available online at www.tda.gov.uk/upload/resources/pdf/s/swdb-1yp.pdf (accessed 22 March 2008).

Training and Development Agency (TDA) (2006) *Developing People to Support Learning: A skills strategy for the wider school workforce 2006–09.* Available online at www.tda.gov.uk/support/swdb/swdb2006to09.aspx (accessed 22 October 2007).

Training and Development Agency (TDA) (2007) *Higher Level Teaching Assistants.* Available online at www.tda.gov.uk/support/hlta.aspx (accessed 5 February 2008).

FURTHER READING

Rose, R. (2005) *Becoming a Primary Higher Level Teaching Assistant.* Exeter: Learning Matters.

3 WORKING WITH OTHER PROFESSIONALS

Susan Graves

CHAPTER OBJECTIVES

By the end of this chapter you will:

- be able to discuss a number of strategies and initiatives that impact on the development of the children's workforce in schools;
- appreciate how integrated assessment and inspection frameworks are impacting on the development of integrated working;
- understand how an integrated children's workforce is developing;
- appreciate the benefits and challenges of multi-agency, multi-professional working and some of the skills needed for successful team working.

LINKS TO **HLTA** STANDARDS

1. Communicate effectively and sensitively with children, young people, colleagues, parents and carers.
2. Demonstrate a commitment to collaborative and co-operative working with colleagues.
3. Know how other frameworks, which support the development and well-being of children and young people, impact upon their practice.
4. Contribute to maintaining and analysing records of learners' progress.
5. Direct the work, where relevant, of other adults in supporting learning.

Introduction

This chapter will look at the development of an integrated workforce as a key aspect of the government's strategy for the provision of children's services and the Change for Children agenda in the UK. It will look at the benefits and challenges of multi-agency, multi-professional working in the development of an integrated children's workforce. Additionally, it will examine how the development of an Integrated Qualifications Framework (IQF) and Common Core of Skills and Knowledge for this workforce is intended to align professionals' work more collaboratively. The development of children's centres and extended schools will also be discussed, along with the Common Assessment and Integrated Inspection Frameworks that are intended to ensure that services move away from being professional silos, and become interdependent and inter-reliant in terms of monitoring and improving children's services.

Developing the school workforce

Background

The reform of the school workforce is part of a larger government agenda that will develop integrated services for children. The intention is that services in terms of education, health and social services will be offered in a more cohesive manner to children and their families, possibly from a single site. There are also plans to increase provision through extended schools, expand the school curriculum, introduce more personalised learning and change testing and examinations at all levels.

These long-term aims will inevitably mean changes to the way in which schools operate and to the roles of those who work in them. Change is an inevitable part of organisation life in the twenty-first century and nowhere is this more in evidence than in the educational world. Government initiatives and policies over the last ten years have seen some of the most radical changes in the way schools are managed and funded, in the design, delivery and testing of the curriculum and in the profile of staff working within the classroom. For those working in schools, the ability to adapt and deal with this change from both professional and personal points of view is vital.

From the perspective of schools, it is those schools that are able to adopt and adapt new initiatives to their own context, grasp opportunities to enhance funding, for example through special funding grants, and maximise the potential of the whole workforce, that will be able to survive and thrive in the future.

Developing support staff

The development of support staff in schools is a key feature of the government's Remodelling agenda, with the twin aims of enhancing learning within the classroom and ensuring that the changes to teachers' contracts – designed to enhance their work/life balance and give time within the school day for preparation, planning and assessment – are implemented within every school. This was set out in the National Workforce Agreement, which was signed by ministers on 15 January 2003. This is a national agreement with key partners, including local authority employers and some school workforce unions, which laid out statutory contractual conditions under which teachers would be employed with a view to a progressive reduction in teachers' overall hours. A timetable for implementation was included, which gave deadlines for instigating a concerted attack on unnecessary paperwork and bureaucratic processes, additional resources and a national change management programme and reform of support staff roles (DfES, 2003a).

PRACTICAL TASK

Do your own research on the National Workforce Agreement – a starting point is **www.teachernet.gov.uk**.

The National Workforce Agreement

The agreement was informed by the Teacher Workload study, which had been undertaken by PriceWaterhouseCoopers and reported in December 2001 (PWC, 2001). This study looked at workloads for teachers and other staff in schools nationally and made recommendations for future staffing policy in schools based on the research. The recommendations included strategies to reduce teachers' overall working hours by deploying support staff in more enhanced roles within classrooms alongside the introduction of guaranteed non-contact time for teachers. They foresaw the latter being managed through *a mix of increased use of supply staff; recruitment of additional teaching staff; supporting learning through staff other than teachers; and/or supporting learning using ICT* (ibid., p105). They acknowledged within the report that using support staff in enhanced classroom roles was of concern to many on educational grounds and, though they were broadly supportive of the introduction of the para-professional role for support staff, agreed that *the rationale [for using support staff in the classroom] must clearly be established on grounds of quality and on better use of staffing resources* (ibid., p44).

In September 2002, a pilot of the Workforce Agreement was implemented with 32 Pathfinder schools, which were geographically spread across England to include urban and rural settings and primary and secondary sectors. These schools went through a five-stage change process led by a school change team and were given extra funding of £4 million from government collectively to pilot the initiative. These were followed in 2003 by 189 Early Adopter schools who implemented the agreement before others, to test out the thinking. These Early Adopter schools were not given any additional funding to carry out this work. Support for the implementation of the Workforce Agreement was provided through the National Remodelling Team (NRT) led by Dame Patricia Collarbone, director of leadership and development programmes at the National College for School Leadership (NCL). The NRT's remit was to support the creation of a national network of support to help schools implement workforce reform. Subsequently, local Workforce Agreement Monitoring Groups (WAMGs) were set up to include signatories to the agreement (e.g. local authority employers and some school workforce unions) to monitor implementation at a local level reporting to NRT.

A publication from Ofsted, entitled *Reforming and Developing the School Workforce*, published in October 2007, reported that almost all the schools visited had met the statutory requirements of the national agreement and that the reforms have resulted in a revolutionary shift in workforce culture with clear benefits for many of the schools. It also reported that the substantial expansion of the wider workforce in schools, and the increasing breadth and diversity of roles, were leading to changes in working practices at all levels in the schools surveyed. Additionally, the report claimed that pupils benefited from increased support from members of the wider workforce, as deploying adults with different skills allowed the schools to improve care and guidance for vulnerable pupils and those at risk of exclusion.

However, this report also suggested that the full potential of the wider workforce to raise achievement and standards was not realised when schools did not match skills and expertise sufficiently closely to school needs, and when insufficient attention was given to the performance management and career development of the workforce.

> **REFLECTIVE TASK**
> Consider the deployment of support staff in your school and see if you can make the links with policy as outlined above.

Other national drivers

There are other national drivers that are significant in developing an enhanced role for support staff in schools. The Government Spending Review 2002 announced key reforms that will have an impact on staffing in all schools, both primary and secondary. The document entitled *Investment for Reform* contained the following initiatives that will impact on support staff.

- *In early years the establishment of new Children's Centres to cover up to 650,000 children by 2006 providing childcare, early years education and health and family services for deprived communities.*
- *Enrichment of the primary curriculum – extra PE and sporting activities, music and modern foreign languages – to provide access to a broad and varied curriculum.*
- *Expansion of extended schools that co-locate services for deprived communities and provide all day schooling and childcare.*
- *Enhanced take-up of sporting opportunities by 5–16 year olds, increasing the percentage of children who spend at least 2 hours each week on PE and school sport within and beyond the curriculum to 75% by 2006.*
- *A major drive on specialisation . . . every [secondary] school to aim for specialist status with a distinctive mission and centre of excellence.*

(DfES, 2002)

All of the above initiatives will have an effect on the staffing policies within schools and one can see how experienced, well-qualified support staff could be used to staff, in particular, the extended schools and children's centres. The development of specialist teaching assistants to work alongside teachers to develop the enriched curriculum for primary schools, the specialist secondary schools and the extension of sport and PE across both sectors would seem to be a logical step. Indeed the TDA is at the moment piloting HLTA training for specialist routes in languages and sport, which will fit alongside specialisms in maths and science.

Changing to the remit of schools in terms of offering extended services to pupils, parents and the local community will also impact on the staffing requirements in schools. The following case study looks at how a cluster of schools in East Yorkshire is developing a wide range of extended services to its local community and some of the impact that has on staffing within the school.

CASE STUDY 1

South Hunsley is a large secondary school in East Yorkshire that offers a wide range of extended services to its community and its cluster of eight primary schools. The school is open all year round from 7 a.m. until 10 p.m. on weekdays, from 7 a.m. until 5 p.m. on Saturdays and from 8 a.m. to 5 p.m. on Sundays. An extensive range of clubs and activities is offered from 4 p.m. until 6 p.m. 'We had to radically look at the management structure when we moved to operating for 52 weeks a year,' says headteacher Chris Abbott, 'because some of the school's staff are only available in term time. Everything has changed from the model we had.' The decision to give the heads of year role to non-teaching staff was taken to improve swift and easy referral and the general level of pastoral care. 'The associate heads of year are the points of contact for parents and outside agencies and providers,' says Chris. 'A teaching head of year can be hard to get hold of, so with associate heads of year we are able to deal with issues quickly and offer parents instant access.' The associate heads of year carry both mobile phones and radios.

The school holds regular multi-agency partner meetings at its lifelong learning centre. The meetings include representatives from Connexions, the police, health, behaviour support, youth services, the education welfare service and educational psychologists, as well as the school's own key stage directors and its non-teaching heads of year. All attendees were involved in a developing and agreeing a protocol for dealing with referrals. The school has also developed a booklet for staff that provides information about partner agencies and the referral process, and one for sixth-form pupils.

As well as providing support for individual pupils and their families, agencies work with the school to run a range of activities. Connexions and youth services help to run South Hunsley's Monday morning breakfast club, with input from drugs workers, the school nurse, family support workers, the trainee social worker, the education welfare officer and the extended schools co-ordinator. At the end of each ten-week block of activities, an awards ceremony is held to celebrate pupils' achievements.

Youth services support an after-school club for Year 7 pupils, which includes a homework zone, movie club, sports activities and cooking. The school is also working with adult education to offer family learning courses linked to its specialism in engineering and technology, which have proved very popular.

(adapted from TDA website)

REFLECTIVE TASK
- Who are the agencies who are involved in working with pupils and parents in your school?
- What contact do you have with these agencies?
- Who co-ordinates the involvement of outside agencies in your school?

The 14–19 agenda

The numbers of young people not in education, employment or training (known as NEETs) in the 14–19 bracket have been of concern to government in recent years.

In an effort to address this concern, major reforms to education and training for 14–19 year olds were first set out in February 2005 in *14–19 Education and Skills* (DCSF, 2005), which was followed by a 14–19 implementation plan in December of the same year. Some modifications and developments to the initial proposals followed, culminating in a new consultation document in March 2008, *Promoting Achievement, Valuing Success: A strategy for 14–19 qualifications* (DCSF, 2008).

The strategy advocates a new broad curriculum for the 14–19-year-old age group, which includes vocational pathways delivered through flexible, integrated programmes that young people can access through a variety of providers. There are also proposals for clear vocational pathways to higher education to be developed that would give young people undertaking work-related programmes and apprenticeships a clear progression to degree programmes, which will extend their practical competence and also give a sound academic underpinning (DCSF, 2008).

PRACTICAL TASK

Look at the report, *Promoting Achievement, Valuing Success: A strategy for 14–19 qualifications* (DCSF, 2008) at **www.dcsf.gov.uk/publications/14–19qualifications/**.

Make a list of the staff who are potentially involved in successfully delivering this strategy for young people at the local level.

We can see, if we reflect on the above, that the role of enhanced support staff in schools supporting teachers with these initiatives plays a crucial part in linking together the various agencies and staff who will be working towards ensuring the best possible outcomes for pupils. In these circumstances, the staffing policy of the whole school needs to be examined to ensure that the necessary skills and experience are developed across the whole workforce in terms of access to professional and career development.

It also has to be acknowledged that there is some distrust and disquiet within the teaching profession concerning the enhanced role of TAs that is proposed within the Remodelling agenda. This is particularly apparent concerning the role of the new HLTA, who can, if the head is in agreement, be left in sole charge of a class. In the summer of 2003, there was a very well-publicised campaign by the National Union of Teachers (NUT) (who are not signatories to the National Agreement or part of the Workforce Agreement Monitoring Group) under the heading 'Who is teaching your child today?', which sought to argue that the use of TAs in classrooms was something parents should oppose on the grounds that it would disadvantage their children (NUT, 2003). Some teachers feel that the profession has had to work hard to ensure an all-graduate teaching force and to keep pupil/teacher ratio within reasonable limits (TES, 2004). There is suspicion also that, although at the moment the agenda is very clear with teaching assistants required to work under the direct supervision of a qualified teacher, a future government or minister may use the Remodelling process to replace teachers with assistants on a much lower salary. This issue of professionalism and how overlapping and new roles are managed in the change process, makes us realise that at the heart of this Remodelling agenda are people having to make, sometimes, painful and difficult adjustments to their own perceptions of their professional role.

REFLECTIVE TASK

List some of the challenges and benefits in terms of developing the role of support staff within the school workforce.

Developing an integrated children's workforce

This section looks at some of the issues in developing an integrated workforce for children.

Background

The concept of an integrated workforce for children's services is, in part, a result of the Laming Report (2003), which reported on the Victoria Climbié scandal .This report has had an important impact on children's policy, as the findings identified serious failures in the lack of communication and collaboration between professionals across healthcare, education, police and social services, which, it was felt, resulted in the tragic death of the five year old.

The Every Child Matters agenda

The major government initiative that is driving these developments is *Every Child Matters: Change for children*, with its five aims:

> *that every child, whatever their background or their circumstances, will have the support they need to:*
> - *Be healthy*
> - *Stay safe*
> - *Enjoy and achieve*
> - *Make a positive contribution*
> - *Achieve economic well-being.*

(DfES, 2003a)

This is informing the structure and operation of the new children's services in terms of policy, service provision and workforce education. To develop a workforce that will be able to meet the requirements of the *Every Child Matters* policy, the *Children's Workforce Strategy* set out the requirements in terms of developing a workforce that:

- *strives to achieve the best possible outcomes for all children and young people;*
- *is competent, confident and safe to work with children and young people;*
- *[people] aspire to be part of and want to remain in – where they can develop their skills and build satisfying and rewarding careers; and*
- *parents, children and young people trust and respect.*

(DfES, 2005a, p6)

Common Core of Skills and Knowledge

To help an integrated children's workforce to work together in a consistent and proficient way, a Common Core of Skills and Knowledge has been devised as a requirement for all those working with children. The Common Core has been identified as detailed below.

- Effective communication and engagement with children and young people.
- Child and young person development.
- Safeguarding and promoting the welfare of the child.
- Supporting transitions.

- Multi-agency working.
- Sharing information.

The idea is that all qualifications for those working within the children's workforce would contain the above elements with a common purpose and language. An Integrated Qualifications Framework (IQF) was introduced in 2008, in which all qualifications for those working within the children's workforce will be placed. The development of the Common Core may also allow for progression and transfer of staff between sectors and a better sharing of knowledge and practice across sectors.

Common Assessment Framework

The Common Assessment Framework (CAF) is a standardised approach to conducting an assessment of a child's additional needs and deciding how those needs should be met. It can be used by practitioners from all disciplines who have contact with the child and the intention is that it will promote more effective, earlier identification of additional needs, particularly in universal services. It is intended to provide a simple process for a holistic assessment of a child's needs and strengths, taking account of the roles of parents, carers and environmental factors in their development. Practitioners will then be better placed to agree, with the child and the family, about what support is appropriate. The CAF will also help to improve integrated working by promoting co-ordinated service provision.

Children's centres

Children's centres provide integrated services to children under five and their families, from the antenatal period until children start in reception or Year 1 at primary school. Centres may also offer other services, such as training for parents in terms of parenting classes, basic skills classes or training for work sessions. The intention is that parents will be able to access all the services they may need to support them through the centre and in this way the needs of families can be met in the local community.

Extended schools

The DCSF document, *Extended Schools: Building on experience* (2005b), sets out a core offer of services that all children should be able to access through schools by 2010.

The core offer includes:

- a varied range of activities, including study support, sport and music clubs, combined with childcare in primary schools;
- parenting and family support;
- swift and easy access to targeted and specialist services;
- community access to facilities, including adult and family learning, ICT and sports grounds.

It is intended that schools will work closely with parents, children and others to shape these activities around the needs of their community and may choose to provide extra services in response to demand.

Integrated Inspection Framework

The proposals set out in the *Every Child Matters* green paper, and provided for in the Children Act 2004, prompted new arrangements for inspection of children's services at local authority area level. In future, integrated inspections of children's services will replace inspections of individual services and, it is hoped, will act as a driver to develop joint ways of working within local areas. Services will be monitored through two inspection processes. The first is an annual performance assessment (APA) of each council's children's services. The second is a programme of joint area reviews (JARs), which involve greater depth than the APA and also range beyond council services to include, for example, health and police services. Both processes look at how services are working together locally to improve outcomes for children and young people.

REFLECTIVE TASK
From your experience, what needs to be done locally to ensure that integrated working is implemented effectively?

Benefits of integrated working

- **Earlier, holistic identification of needs** – Being able to identify more completely, accurately and speedily the additional needs of children and young people is the critical first step towards meeting those needs at an early stage and preventing problems escalating.
- **Earlier, more co-ordinated and effective intervention** – Intervening early and in a manner that maximises the available resources (for example, by avoiding duplication of activities, by building on earlier interventions, by working together as a team) secures better outcomes for children. Effective integrated practice is already in place in many areas, for example SureStart, Youth Offending Teams and Drug Action Teams.
- **Improved information sharing across agencies** – Being able to identify other practitioners working with a child or young person and sharing information legally and professionally is vital for early and effective intervention and for safeguarding. Improved practice in information sharing will lead to:
  - more holistic assessment of needs;
  - less duplication of effort;
  - improved understanding of service delivery options;
  - better quality and more appropriate referrals.
- **Better service experience for children and families** – Integrated working will deliver a better service experience that is less stressful to children, young people and families through providing:
  - a child and family-centred approach;
  - improved access to information, advice and support;
  - fewer assessments and less repetition;
  - easier, less bureaucratic access to a range of services;
  - faster access to targeted services and with less stigma as a result of closer links between these targeted services and universal services.
- **Benefits to practitioners and organisations** – In addition, there are also significant benefits for practitioners and organisations in:
  - increased confidence in making decisions about sharing information – due to clearer cross-government guidance;

- less time spent on administrative processes – due to improved access to information on services and practitioners working with children;
- improved access to services through reduced bureaucracy;
- improved quality referrals received – more accurately targeted and more evidence-based.

(adapted from DCSF, 2007)

Challenges of integrated working

Challenges to working in an integrated way with other professionals include the following.

- **Communication barriers** – All professionals have their own language for talking about their work, often referred to as 'jargon'. If others working in the same area are unaware of this jargon, it can present a real barrier to understanding and may in some cases result in real misrepresentation of the facts.
- **Geographical barriers** – Where a service is located may act as a barrier to working with other services in terms of being able to easily meet to discuss issues. The advent of communication technology such as tele-conferencing may help to alleviate this issue.
- **Psychological barriers** – The way professionals in different services think about their work with children may also serve as a barrier to working collaboratively. For example, a teacher may be fully focused on ensuring a pupil attends school to keep up with their GCSE work, whereas the social worker may feel that attendance at family meetings during school time is paramount in terms of looking at the wider issues affecting the child's situation. Talking and working together in an open and holistic way with other professionals can help to overcome some of these difficulties.
- **Competing or conflicting targets** – Issues can be caused when practitioners are working to different targets for the multi-agency service and for their home agencies. There is the potential for these targets to be competing or conflicting, leaving the practitioners confused about what they are supposed to do and potentially in danger of failing to meet one or both of the targets.

> *REFLECTIVE TASK*
> What other challenges can you think of in terms of working across professional boundaries?

Skills for team working

This section looks at some of the skills you may need to develop for team working.

Developing and enhancing the skills needed to work as an effective member of a team is an important aspect of professional development for support staff working within the wider school workforce. These skills include developing oral and written communication skills, time-management and goal-setting skills, problem-solving and conflict-resolution skills. One of the most important skills for ensuring that you develop a good rapport with colleagues is skilful listening, sometimes referred to as active listening. Characteristics of active listening are:

- establishing a calm atmosphere;
- removing or minimising distractions;

- concentrating on the speaker's verbal and physical cues;
- establishing and maintaining positive eye contact;
- using supportive body language – affirmative noises, gestures, facial expressions;
- hearing the message, not just the words;
- showing patience and empathy;
- being aware of and avoiding personal prejudice.

REFLECTIVE TASK

Bearing in mind the above list, monitor your own listening skills over the next few days, both in work and at home – are you an active listener?

PRACTICAL TASK

To assess your own teamwork skills, take the audit below to find out where you may need to develop using the following ratings.

1 = Strongly disagree
2 = Disagree
3 = Not sure
4 = Agree
5 = Strongly agree

Use the results to consider where your development needs are in terms of team working. You should identify where your teamwork performance is not adequate and aim to improve in these areas. A better measure may be to ask your team colleagues to rate you on these dimensions, so you have more objective feedback.

Communication	1	2	3	4	5
I understand and use communication networks, making sufficient contact with colleagues					
I communicate openly and supportively					
I listen actively and non-evaluatively					
There is a consistency between my verbal and non-verbal behaviour					
I value and offer warm greetings and small talk with colleagues					

Goal setting and performance management	1	2	3	4	5
I help establish clear and challenging team goals					
I monitor and give supportive feedback on team and individual performance					

Planning and co-ordination	1	2	3	4	5
I help to co-ordinate activities, information and working together between members					
I help to clarify tasks and roles of team members and ensure balance of workloads					
I respond positively and flexibly to feedback from team members					

Collaborative problem solving	1	2	3	4	5
I identify problems requiring participation of all team members in decision making					
I use appropriate ways of involving team members in decision making					
I explore and support proposals for innovation in the team					

Innovation	1	2	3	4	5
I try to introduce improved methods of doing things at work					
I have ideas that significantly improve the way the job is done					
I suggest new working methods to the people I work with					
I contribute to changes in the way my team works					
I am receptive to new ideas that I can use to improve things in my team					

(adapted from West, 2004)

CHAPTER SUMMARY

- Integrated working with professional colleagues from a variety of disciplines and backgrounds is increasingly the norm.
- Integrated inspection/assessment frameworks mean that developing good working relationships across agencies is vital.
- There are benefits and challenges to working in this way and developing the skills and knowledge to be able to work in teams is essential.
- The role of support staff within schools has expanded massively over recent years.

REFERENCES

Department for Children, Schools and Families (DCSF) (2005) *14–19 Education and Skills*. Available online at www.dcsf.gov.uk/publications/14–19educationandskills/ (accessed 8 October 2008).

Department for Children, Schools and Families (DCSF) (2007) *Integrated Working Training Materials*. Available online at www.everychildmatters.gov.uk/search/IG00062/ (accessed 25 August 2008).

Department for Children, Schools and Families (DCSF) (2008) *Promoting Achievement, Valuing Success: A strategy for 14–19 qualifications*. Available online at www.dcsf.gov.uk/publications/14–19qualifications/ (accessed 8 October 2008).

Department for Education and Skills (DfES) (2002) *Investment for Reform*. London: DfES.

Department for Education and Skills (DfES) (2003a) *Raising Standards and Tackling Workload: A national agreement*. London: DfES.

Department for Education and Skills (DfES) (2003b) *Every Child Matters: Change for children*. Norwich: TSO.

Department for Education and Skills (DfES) (2004) *14–19 Extending Opportunities, Raising Standards*. London: DfES.

Department for Education and Skills (DfES) (2005a) *The Children's Workforce Strategy*. London: DfES.

Department for Education and Skills (DfES) (2005b) *Extended Schools: Building on experience*. London: DfES.

Laming, L. (2003) The Victoria Climbié Inquiry. Available online at www.victoria-climbie-inquiry.org.uk/finreport/report.pdf (accessed 16 January 2009).

National Union of Teachers (NUT) (2003) Who is teaching your child today?, July.

Ofsted (2007) *Reforming and Developing the School Workforce*. London: Ofsted.

PricewaterhouseCoopers (PWC) (2001) *Teacher Workload Study: Final report*. London: DfES.

Times Educational Supplement (TES) (2004) Heads say: you won't pay. Leader, 3 December.

Training and Development Agency (TDA) (2008) *Case Study*. Available online at www.tda.gov.uk/remodelling/extendedschools/esresources/casestudies/remodelling/south_hunsley_new.aspx?itemid={FC4A6EDC-F8E6–4B33-B69F-ECED868211D5} (accessed 24 August 2008).

West, M.A. (2004) *Effective Teamwork: Practical lessons from organisational research* (2nd edn). Oxford: Blackwell.

4 SUPPORTING THE WHOLE CHILD

Maureen Judge and Felix Obadan

CHAPTER OBJECTIVES

By the end of this chapter you will:

- explore aspects of pastoral support and personal, social and health education (PSHE) and citizenship, including social and emotional aspects of learning (SEAL).

- understand the relationship between these aspects and achievement and be able to identify some of the main strategies used to address these needs, such as circle time, one-to-one support, mentoring, peer group support systems, playground activities and thematic topics such as anti-bullying weeks.

- be aware of the various roles support staff can play in these respective fields.

LINKS TO **HLTA** STANDARDS

1. Understand the key factors that affect children's and young people's learning and progress.

2. Know how to contribute to effective personalised provision by taking practical account of diversity.

3. Have sufficient understanding of area(s) of expertise to support the development, learning and progress of children and young people.

4. Know how to support learners in accessing the curriculum in accordance with the special educational needs (SEN) code of practice and disabilities legislation.

5. Know how other frameworks, which support the development and well-being of children and young people, impact upon practice.

6. Plan how to support the inclusion the children and young people in the learning activities.

7. Use effective strategies to promote positive behaviour.

8. Recognise and respond appropriately to situations that challenge equality of opportunity.

9. Organise and manage learning activities in ways that keep learners safe.

It is important to remember that the HLTA standards that address professional attributes link to the objectives in this chapter; however, for further understanding of these, you need to read Chapter 2, which addresses them in depth.

Introduction

This chapter will examine the demands of the Children Act 2004, enshrining the *Every Child Matters* agenda. It will explore aspects of pastoral support and personal, social and health education (PSHE) and citizenship, including social and emotional aspects of learning (SEAL). It will discuss the relationship of these aspects to achievement and will introduce some of the main strategies used to address these needs: circle time, one-to-one support, mentoring, peer group support systems, playground activities and thematic topics such as anti-bullying weeks. It will address the various roles support staff can play in this field.

Background

In September 2003, the government published the green paper called *Every Child Matters* (ECM), which represents *the biggest change to the organisation of provision for children since the 1944 Education Act* (Coombs and Calvert, 2008, p2). This was a result of the response to the inquiry report that looked into the death of a young girl called Victoria Climbié, who was tortured, abused and eventually killed by her great-aunt and the man with whom they lived, and *numerous other child abuse iniquities* (Roche and Tucker, 2007, p213).

The green paper proposed changes in policy and legislation in England to maximise opportunities and minimise risks for all children and young people, focusing services more effectively around the needs of children, young people and families (OPSI, 2007). As stated in Chapter 1, the government's aim was:

> *that every child, whatever their background or their circumstances, will have the support they need to:*
> - *Be healthy*
> - *Stay safe*
> - *Enjoy and achieve*
> - *Make a positive contribution*
> - *Achieve economic wellbeing.*
>
> (DfES, 2008)

Demands of the *Every Child Matters* agenda

To fulfil effectively the demands of the five outcomes of ECM, schools face the challenge of introducing new concepts and ways of working to their structures. Provisions are now made to accommodate activities such as extended schools, personalised learning and healthy schools, as well as expanding the workforce. Coombs and Calvert suggest that staffing in schools has changed dramatically since the remodelling of the workforce, with *now more teaching assistants (TAs) than teachers, not to mention lunchtime supervisors, learning mentors and others in various support roles* (2008, p1). Subsequently, one of the challenges is to ensure that all staff, teaching and non-teaching, are fully aware of the implications of the ECM agenda and the necessity to identify their training requirements in order to meet the needs of the child while addressing the five outcomes of the agenda (Reid, 2005). Roche and Tucker (2007, p220) argue that the training will need to address the *Common Core of Skills and Knowledge for the Children's Workforce* (DfES, 2005), which has six broad areas of expertise, along with meeting the demands of, for example, becoming an extended school.

Pastoral support

In June 2005, as part of the *Excellence and Enjoyment* strategy, the social and emotional aspects of learning (SEAL) programme was launched. The aim of the programme was to provide guidance and curriculum materials for developing children's social, behavioural and emotional skills.

The importance of pastoral support, as documented in the implementation of the Children Act 2004 (OPSI, 2007), reflects a wide range of issues relating to the implementation of the legislation. It also focuses particularly on the challenges faced by schools as they embark upon multi-agency partnerships, and on the ability to develop integrated ways of working with vulnerable children and young people.

Pastoral support systems need to be in place for both pupils and staff. These provide confidential advice and pastoral care, and the provision for these needs affords schools the opportunity to cater for situations such as bereavement and other major life-changing experiences. This helps guard against stigmatisation of and discrimination against such pupils.

Lead professionals have been introduced, such as pastoral staff, who have trusting relationships with the child or parent. These may be in a better position to discuss initial concerns with a child or parent, and work with them over a given period, rather than a social worker with whom the family has had no previous contact. Ongoing curriculum and pastoral support ensures that young people make progress during all learning programmes. Short practical intervention programmes provide support to young persons at risk of disaffection or permanent exclusion. These should be initiated by the school but should be agreed with parents or carers and involve the local authority and other agencies.

Research shows that schools that are most successful in preventing exclusion have policies that tackle underlying causes of poor behaviour with strategies such as pastoral support programmes. Young people in public care usually prefer not to be treated differently from others, but sensitive support, such as that recommended as part of Pastoral Support Programmes (PSPs) or Individual Education Plans (IEPs), can prevent problems as well as deal with any emerging or existing behavioural problems. Pastoral support can include providing a 'buddy' for a child new to the school or the help of a learning mentor or counsellor. Crow (2008) stresses that, according to the Qualifications and Curriculum Authority (QCA), one of the key ways in which a school can show its contribution to the *Every Child Matters* outcomes is through a curriculum that supports personal development and the promotion of well-being.

PRACTICAL TASK
Examine your school policy on PSHE and find out how your school curriculum supports personal development and promotes the well-being of pupils.

Social and emotional aspects of learning

Weare believes that social and emotional learning is *absolutely central to the achievement of ECM* (2007, p239) and agrees with Crow (2008) in that the main aims of social and emotional aspects of learning (SEAL) are to develop skills that encourage children to understand and manage their emotions. The children and young people then need to apply these new skills when interacting and building relationships with others. In addition, Crow draws our attention to the challenges and demands of implementing SEAL, one being the curriculum congestion and:

> *[the] lack of an underlying or clearly unifying rationale for PSHE or SEAL, both of which are perceived as tapping into broadly the same vein – something about 'emotions' but not subject learning.*
>
> (2008, p48)

Another possible challenge might be teachers' lack of confidence in delivering this aspect of the curriculum.

SEAL is described by Crow (2008) as a whole-school approach with a curriculum focus, which can be clearly seen in Morrison and Matthews' research into 'How pupils can be helped to develop socially and emotionally in science lessons' (2006). Their belief is that, if teachers incorporated elements of pastoral work into their teaching through collaborative group work, it would reduce the conflict in class rather than keeping it as a separate issue normally addressed by the form tutor.

The researchers draw our attention to work by Megahy (cited in Morrison and Matthews, 2006), who states that attention to pastoral care can improve achievement. Arguably, the results from the research clearly show this to be true. The research consisted of classes where groups made up of two boys and two girls were encouraged to work together and discuss their work.

The class teachers who took part in the research gave very positive comments on how the pupils' behaviour had improved, with less conflict, especially between the boys, who were even *willing to engage with their emotions* (ibid., p15). Pupils were more disposed to work collaboratively in mixed-gender groups and contribute to the lesson without fear of ridicule by their peers. The difference in the research classes and the control class was that the control class had not developed support systems. An interesting observation by the class teachers was that, even after the research had finished, pupils who joined the research groups appeared subconsciously to recognise the social and emotional behaviour of the other pupils and to conform.

Greenhalgh (1994) supports this view, highlighting that emotional development is a key aspect in enabling pupils to learn, and that pupils can become more effective learners when they develop emotionally. Steiner (1997) defined emotional literacy as:

> *the ability to understand your emotions, the ability to listen to others and empathise with their emotions, and the ability to express emotions productively.*
>
> *Emotional literacy improves relationships . . . [and] . . . makes co-operative work possible.*
> (cited in Morrison and Matthews, 2006, p11)

There are many definitions of emotional literacy, however; the definition by the organisation Antidote (2003) states that:

> *Emotional Literacy is the practice of thinking individually and collectively about how emotions shape our actions, and of using emotional understanding to enrich our thinking.*
> (cited in Morrison and Matthews, 2006, p11)

This view suggests that, if children have a better understanding of their emotions, their behaviour will improve and this will also impact on their learning. Furthermore, Radcliffe agrees by highlighting the importance of developing emotional literacy in *helping children make the link between emotional feelings, thinking and behaviour* (2008, p1). Consequently, the teacher has an important role to play in promoting this aptitude and will benefit directly from its application in his or her classroom.

Additionally, Radcliffe (2008) suggests that a good way to implement SEAL across the whole school is through assemblies. This addresses the need for whole-school ownership of the underpinning values espoused by the programme.

REFLECTIVE TASK
How might emotional literacy improve behaviour and combat bullying in schools?

Bullying

Bullying is a form of poor behaviour that causes particular unhappiness and disruption to the learning of individual pupils. Anyone can experience bullying, but there is evidence that some groups, including disabled children and looked-after children, are more likely to be bullied than others.

Schools should have a policy to prevent bullying among pupils and must make sure that it is in line with the Human Rights Act 1998. Anti-bullying policies should:

- identify the extent and nature of bullying that takes place in schools;
- raise the profile of bullying and its effects on children and young people's emotional health and well-being, life chances and achievement;
- establish a culture where bullying is not acceptable, through the promotion of policies and practices that prevent or reduce opportunities for bullying to occur, and deal swiftly, fairly and sensitively when they do;
- involve parents, carers, children and young people in developing and implementing anti-bullying strategies;
- embody equality of opportunity, celebrate diversity and be responsive to individual needs and differences.

This policy also needs to recognise the particular vulnerability of looked-after children. It should be monitored by the governing body of the school as it shows how concerned they are about pupils' health and safety. The governing body should ensure that the school's anti-bullying and behaviour policies are flexible in their understanding of care issues and support early intervention. The school must inform pupils, in particular looked-after children, so that they understand the process for making complaints.

PRACTICAL TASK
Locate and read your school anti-bullying policy to see if the above points are included within the policy. Does the policy need updating? Do you know what the procedure is if a child informs you that they are being bullied?

REFLECTIVE TASK
What could be done to ensure that pupils are not too frightened to speak out and ask for help?

Mellor and Munn (2000) suggest that circle time can have a major impact on young people by promoting respect for others and, therefore, has a significant role in the prevention of bullying.

What is circle time?

Although circle time has been practised in many primary schools since Jenny Mosley first introduced it in the 1990s, it is only recently that secondary schools are recognising the benefits. Circle time is designed to address behavioural, social and emotional problems for children in a safe and secure environment.

The circle time model is a whole-school approach and, therefore, all staff need to be involved in order to maintain a *positive school management system* to:

- *promote positive behavior;*
- *create a caring and respectful school ethos;*
- *help children develop their self-esteem and self-confidence;*
- *provide efficient and effective systems and support for staff;*
- *create great lunchtimes and playtimes;*
- *nurture the creativity in all people in school.*

(Mosley, 2008, p1)

It can be seen from the above that circle time will help schools to address all five outcomes from the Children Act 2004 and the ECM agenda. The sessions can be linked to PSHE and citizenship. Bell states that *[a] school providing good citizenship education is also doing well in terms of the* Every Child Matters *agenda* (cited in Warwick, 2007, p261). Circle time involves weekly sessions of approximately half an hour with the teacher or teaching assistant sitting in a circle with the pupils and includes activities, games and the practice of speaking and listening skills, often in a round. The key elements are:

- *improving the morale and self-esteem of staff;*
- *listening systems for children and adults;*
- *the Golden Rules: a system of behavioural rules for children;*
- *incentives: a weekly celebration to congratulate the children for keeping the Golden Rules;*

- *sanctions: the partial withdrawal of the Golden Time incentive;*
- *[a] lunchtime policy.*

(ibid.)

Many TAs are either included in quality circle time or run the session themselves; therefore, the need for consistency is very important. Circle time has clear set ground rules that must be adhered to if it is going to be successful, with children understanding the consequences if the rules are broken.

REFLECTIVE TASK

Does your school use circle time as a whole-school approach? If so, list the benefits for the pupil, the class teacher and the school.

CASE STUDY 1

Sarah, a teaching assistant employed in a primary school, was working very closely with a Year 1 child named Mary, who was very quiet, had low self-esteem and was reluctant to speak to any adults or even her peers. The lunchtime supervisor had also noticed her reluctance to join in any activities and saw her very often walking around the playground on her own. The class teacher was finding it very difficult to assess Mary's level of attainment fully and was very concerned about her social and emotional development. Sarah was asked to work with the pupil to encourage her to communicate and join in lunchtime activities.

REFLECTIVE TASK

How would you work with this pupil to help her overcome her difficulties? Make a list of the strategies you would employ and the activities you might include. Now read the teaching assistant response.

Teaching assistant response

Sarah observed Mary by sitting with the group that she was working in. She appeared to be coping well with the work set by the class teacher and on occasion spoke very quietly to one particular pupil, Clare, if she was stuck. This was reassuring and Sarah immediately decided to try to develop this communication into a friendship that would hopefully develop her confidence, social skills and self-esteem. Sarah organised the pupils into pairs to work on number and phonic activities and encouraged them to explain their strategies and results. At first, Mary was very reluctant to speak when she thought anyone other than Clare was listening. Sarah had a great deal of information on circle time and its benefits in developing pupils' social and emotional skills, so she approached the class teacher and suggested that she try this with Mary's group before introducing it to the whole class. The class teacher agreed, so Sarah found a quiet area, sat with the pupils and explained the rules of circle time and that they should only speak when it was their turn and they were holding the teddy bear. Sarah assured Mary that she only needed to talk if she wanted to and, if she didn't, she just needed to say 'pass'. She introduced an activity called 'Rounds' because the learning aims were:

- *to share feelings;*
- *to evaluate experience;*
- *to develop talking and listening.*

Sarah felt that this activity would not only address Mary's needs but would also develop the social and emotional skills of the other members of the group. The activity involved the pupils finishing the sentence 'I feel happy when . . .' to encourage them to share their feelings. She decided to focus on a happy occasion first to gain their confidence and ensure that they enjoyed the activity. As expected, Mary didn't speak on the first round, so Sarah tried again and asked the pupils to think of another time when they felt happy. The other pupils asked Mary to join in and share her 'happy times', as one pupil put it. At first, she struggled getting the words out but it was a start. The group continued to have circle time once a week and, after six weeks, Mary was starting to open up and talk to the group. The class teacher had noticed her increased confidence in class when she was working with the group, so decided to continue with circle time and was keen to introduce it to the whole class, with which Mary coped well. The friendship developed between Mary and Clare, extending to after school. Mary is still quiet but has much more confidence in class, contributing to discussion and joining in activities in the playground. The lunchtime supervisor says that Mary is a happy little girl now and it's good to see her joining in and having fun.

REFLECTIVE TASK

Compare your ideas/strategies with the TA in case study 1. Were any of your strategies and activities the same? Would you have used a different approach and, if so, why?

One-to-one support

There are many reasons why a child might be given one-to-one support, ranging from medical to behavioural or individual learning needs. Each case is assessed on its own merits and the provision that is put in place depends on the severity of assistance the child needs. This can be provided by the local authority, if the child has a statement of SEN, or the school, depending on the reason for the support. The support staff who work with these children play a very special role in helping them overcome barriers to their learning, develop their self-esteem and raise their academic achievement.

PRACTICAL TASK

Consider the ways in which a learning support assistant (LSA), special support assistant (SSA) or TA can provide direct one-to-one pupil support. Use the diagram below to list the tasks they might perform.

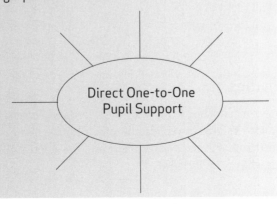

CASE STUDY 2

Stephen is 12 years old and has moderate learning difficulties and behavioural problems. He achieved below average marks in Year 6 National Tests and has, therefore, been granted one-to-one support in secondary school for core subjects. The aim of the LSA is to monitor Stephen's behaviour in lessons and develop strategies to keep him focused and on task. He is very disruptive and argumentative towards his peers and disrespectful to his class teachers. Consequently, he is often removed from class, put on a report card and given detention.

REFLECTIVE TASK

If you were the LSA assigned to Stephen, what strategies would you employ to improve his behaviour and encourage him to work co-operatively in lessons?

Learning support assistant response

When meeting Stephen for the first time, he wouldn't speak to me and when he eventually did he was argumentative and aggressive. However, I explained that I'd be supporting him in particular lessons and my aim was to help him remain in class and stay focused on his lessons, which would stop him getting detention and being on a report card. I found that, in lessons, Stephen didn't always follow the teacher's instructions, simply because he didn't understand. He became very frustrated with himself and this manifested itself in very poor behavior. Subsequently, I set down some ground rules with Stephen in line with the school's behaviour policy, and told him that I could help explain the teacher's instructions if he didn't understand them. I was able to explain what the teacher wanted in a way that Stephen could understand and also break the work down into manageable steps, helping him to achieve and building his self-esteem. If Stephen's concentration lapsed, I either spoke his name or asked him a question to help him refocus, which allowed him to complete work and even answer questions. Once Stephen's self-esteem improved, his behaviour began to improve also, but I realised it would take quite a while to gain Stephen's trust completely. I hope to instil in Stephen the need to take responsibility for his actions and the need to talk about his feelings, rather than just reacting with hostility in certain situations. I'm happy with the progress Stephen is making but we still have a long way to go.

PRACTICAL TASK

The LSA is making links to citizenship, in which the child needs to take responsibility for their own behaviour. Locate the school PSHE and citizenship policy and identify other strategies that can be used to help children like Stephen. Then reflect on what, if anything, you would do differently?

Playground activities

Teachernet (2008) draws our attention to the fact that *children spend around 25 per cent of their school day in the playground*. This can be very daunting for a number of children and young people who are excluded from activities that, in many cases, are dominated by a small number of children who decide who can be 'included'.

PRACTICAL TASK

Make a list of all the playground activities that you or the lunchtime supervisor organise and do with the children.

The government and the Youth Sport Trust have been working together since 2001 on a three-phase project called 'Zoneparc' to try to overcome the problem and ensure that playgrounds are active, exhilarating, safe and secure places for all. Zoneparc is just one of the projects that the Youth Sport Trust is promoting that address the five outcomes of the ECM agenda. It is a primary playground project aimed at making playtimes safer and children more active, while tackling social exclusion and improving behaviour.

One of the approaches they promote is the division of play space into areas for different activities, for example a quiet play area for reading and talking, a sports area, preferably fenced for fast-flowing min-sports or ball games, and a general play area, possibly incorporating a 'stage' for pupil-led performances of dance and theatre. Many primary school playgrounds now incorporate this type of zoning. Supervision can be an issue, with few lunchtime assistants available; however, if the dynamic and extremely physical activities are organised and supervised separately, it is probable that the other areas will have many fewer incidents requiring intervention.

What is important here is for schools to acknowledge the significance of playtime as a means of developing the whole child, rather than leaving it as a 'non-learning' time that frequently may be boring and, at times, actively harmful to the pupils. This type of activity can improve pupils' well-being by building their self-esteem and influencing or even changing their attitudes to learning, breaking down barriers and providing them with a brighter future. It reduces lunch- and playtime trouble too, and that is something of benefit to all school staff.

REFLECTIVE TASK

In what ways does your school lunchtime organisation or supervision promote positive behaviour, healthy lifestyles and personal and social learning?

Many lunchtime supervisors are also TAs and are in a very privileged position to help identify the early signs of problems that children may be experiencing. They also to have the opportunity to influence the children's future and help and guide them in becoming model citizens, taking responsibility for their own actions. They are a key part of the school staff and need to be acknowledged and valued as such.

CHAPTER SUMMARY

- There are demands and challenges inherent in the ECM agenda for schools that are introducing new initiatives to address the five outcomes of the Children Act 2004.

- The role of support staff is continually changing and there is a need to keep up to date with new initiatives and legislation.
- All staff, teaching or non-teaching, can make a difference and have an impact on a child's life and future.

REFERENCES

Coombs, S. and Calvert, M. (2008) *Every Child Matters: Challenges and opportunities for CPD.* Available online at www.teachingexpertise.com/articles/every-child-matters-challenges-and-opportunities -for-cpd-3233 (accessed 2 September 2008).

Crow, F. (2008) Learning for well being: personal, social and health education and a changing curriculum. *Pastoral Care in Education*, 26(1): 43–51.

Department for Education and Skills (DfES) (2005) *Common Core of Skills and Knowledge for the Children's Workforce.* London: DfES.

Department for Education and Skills (DfES) (2008) *Outcomes for Children and Young People.* Available online at www.everychildmatters.gov.uk/aims/outcomes/ (accessed 25 August 2008).

Greenhalgh, P.(1994) *Emotional Growth and Learning.* London: Routledge.

Mellor, A.and Munn, P. (2000) *Information on Circle Time.* Available online at www.antibullying.net/circletimeinfo.htm (accessed 22 October 2008).

Morrison, L. and Matthews, B. (2006) How pupils can be helped to develop socially and emotionally in science lessons. *Pastoral Care*, 24(1): 10–19.

Mosley, J. (2008) *What is Quality Circle Time.* Available online at www.circle-time.co.uk/site/what_is_quality_circle_time (accessed 25 August 2008).

Office of Public Sector Information (OPSI) (2007) *Explanatory Notes to the Children Act 2004.* Available online at www.opsi.gov.uk/acts/acts2004/en/ukpgaen_20040031_en.pdf (accessed 24 August 2008).

Reid, K. (2005) The implications of *Every Child Matters* and the Children Act for schools. *Pastoral Care*, 23(1): 12–18.

Roche, J. and Tucker, S. (2007) *Every Child Matters*: 'tinkering' or 'reforming' – an analysis of the development of the Children Act (2004) from an educational perspective. *Education 3–13*, 35(3): 213–23.

teachernet (2008) *Sporting Playgrounds.* Available online at www.teachernet.gov.uk/teachingand learning/subjects/pe/nationalstrategy/Sporting_Playgrounds/ (accessed 4 October 2008).

Training and Development Agency (TDA) (2008) *HLTA Standards.* Available online at www.tda.gov.uk/support/hlta/professstandards.aspx (accessed 15 August 2008).

Warwick, P. (2007) Hearing pupils' voices: revealing the need for citizenship education within primary schools. *Education 3–13*, 35(3): 261–72.

Weare, K. (2007) Delivering *Every Child Matters:* the central role of social and emotional learning in schools. *Education 3–13*, 35(3): 239–48.

Youth Sports Trust (2008) *Zoneparc.* Available online at www.youthsporttrust.org/page/zp/index.html (accessed 17 September 2008).

FURTHER READING

Lorenz, S. (2002) *Effective In-class Support.* London: David Fulton Publishers.

5 INCLUSION

Linda Dunne

CHAPTER OBJECTIVES

By the end of this chapter you will:

- gain an understanding of the historical context and development of inclusive education;
- be more critically aware of the concept and nature of inclusion;
- reflect upon how you can enhance inclusive practice and contribute to an inclusive ethos and culture.

LINKS TO **HLTA** STANDARDS

1. Understand the key factors that affect children's and young people's learning and progress.

2. Know how to contribute to effective personalised provision by taking practical account of diversity.

3. Know how to support learners in accessing the curriculum in accordance with the special educational needs (SEN) code of practice and disabilities legislation.

4. Plan how to support the inclusion of the children and young people in learning activities.

5. Recognise and respond appropriately to situations that challenge equality of opportunity.

6. Organise and manage learning activities in ways that keep learners safe.

Introduction

The role of teaching assistants (TAs) in supporting teaching and learning, and the way in which that support is provided, have been seen to be crucial to the inclusion process in schools (Sorsby, 2004; Richards and Armstrong, 2008). This chapter considers the concept and practice of inclusion. It will encourage you to reflect upon inclusion, on what it means and on how you can enhance the inclusive practice and culture of your workplace.

Inclusive school reform

Inclusion may be seen as a concept, or an idea, that suggests that nobody is excluded. It seems to be something that has 'always been there' and it has become part of taken-for-granted everyday practices in schools. However, inclusive school reform has a history that has shaped where we are today.

Originally, inclusion was offered as a protest and a call for radical change to the fabric of schooling. The Salamanca Statement (UNESCO, 1994) pressed for international moves towards inclusion based on rights, recognition and entitlement for all children. The first significant UK policies that emphasised inclusion in education were *Excellence for All Children: Meeting special educational needs* (DfEE, 1997) and the subsequent *Meeting SEN: A programme of action* (DfEE, 1998). It was these particular UK policies that called for greater moves towards inclusion and for an increase in the number of TAs working in schools to assist teaching and learning and to meet learning needs.

The National Curriculum was subsequently modified in 1999 to acknowledge inclusion. The Curriculum is the starting point for planning a school curriculum that meets the specific needs of individuals and groups of learners. It contains a statutory inclusion statement on providing effective learning opportunities for *all* pupils and outlines how teachers can modify the National Curriculum as necessary, to provide all children with relevant and appropriately challenging work at each key stage. The National Curriculum is formulated upon three core inclusion-oriented principles.

1. Setting suitable learning challenges.
2. Responding to pupils' diverse needs.
3. Overcoming potential barriers to learning and assessment for individuals and groups of children.

Planning for inclusion addresses the three inclusion principles (see Figure 5.1) by drawing on:

- a range of access strategies;
- varied teaching styles;
- appropriate learning objectives.

As the following timeline on page 55 shows, the beginning of the twenty-first century saw further policies, initiatives and legislation that called for increased inclusion. For example, the Special Educational Needs and Disability Act (HM Government, 2001); the *Every Child Matters* agenda (DfES, 2003) and the government's strategy for SEN, *Removing Barriers to Achievement* (DfES, 2004) all strengthened moves towards inclusion.

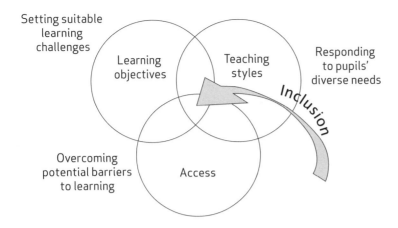

Figure 5.1: The circles of inclusion (www.standards.dfes.gov.uk).

A timeline of significant legislation and initiatives relating to inclusion in education

1978   Warnock Report. Introduced term 'special educational needs' (SEN) and a 'continuum' of need.

1981   Education Act. Definitions of SEN.

1988   Education Reform Act. Right of all children to access a broad and balanced curriculum.

1994   Salamanca Statement. International moves towards inclusion based on rights and entitlement for all children.

1994   *Code of Practice on the Identification and Assessment of Pupils with SEN.* A five-stage guidance model for schools.

1995   Disability Discrimination Act.

1996   Education Act. Strengthened children's rights to be educated in mainstream schools.

1997   *Excellence for All Children: Meeting SEN.* Introduced term 'inclusion'.

1998   *Meeting SEN: A programme of action.* Aimed at developing more inclusive approaches.

2000   Revised National Curriculum. Formulated upon three core inclusion-oriented principles: setting suitable learning challenges, responding to pupils' diverse needs and overcoming potential barriers to learning and assessment for individuals and groups of children.

2000   *Index for Inclusion.* Inclusive indicators and support for schools in developing inclusion.

2001   Revised *Code of Practice.*

2001   Special Educational Needs and Disability Act.

2001   *Inclusive Schooling.* Guidelines for developing effective inclusion.

2003   *Every Child Matters: Change for children.* Sets out the future direction of services working around children.

2004   The Children Act. Provides the legislative spine of *Every Child Matters.*

2004   *Removing Barriers to Achievement.* Government strategy for SEN and inclusion.

2007   *Inclusion Development Programme.* Early intervention and strategic approaches.

Inclusion is an unending process that involves change and improvement. Over the course of continuous educational reform, it remains predominant in the present UK government's educational policy and school improvement agenda (DfES, 2007). The aims behind many of the more recent inclusive education policy initiatives have been to:

- improve the outcomes for all pupils and to narrow the gaps between the lowest and highest achievers;
- promote early recognition and intervention;
- increase the confidence of all practitioners (teachers and teaching assistants);
- support schools and settings to be more effective at strategic approaches to support and intervention.

PRACTICAL TASK

Each school will have its own policy that relates to inclusion. Find out about your school's inclusion policy.

REFLECTIVE TASK

Reflect upon the three principles of inclusion as presented in the National Curriculum statutory inclusion statement.

- A range of access strategies.
- Varied teaching styles.
- Appropriate learning objectives.

How and to what extent do these principles underpin your approach to working with children?

What is inclusion?

So far, we have looked at the historical policy development of inclusion. But what exactly does inclusion mean? Despite its infusion in policy and references to participation, meeting diverse needs and so on, there is no single shared definition of inclusion and it is wide open to different meanings and interpretations. Some researchers and organisational bodies do offer definitions of what inclusion is or what it ought to be. For example, Ofsted, the school inspectorate, offers this definition:

Educational inclusion . . . is about equal opportunities for all pupils . . . it pays particular attention to the provision for, and achievement of, different groups of pupils.

(Ofsted, 2001)

Ofsted's definition of 'groups' is:

- girls and boys, men and women;
- black and minority ethnic and faith groups;
- travellers;
- asylum seekers and refugees;

- learners with 'special educational needs';
- 'gifted and talented' learners;
- children 'looked after' by the local authority;
- sick children;
- young carers;
- children from families under stress;
- learners at risk of disaffection and exclusion.

The Centre for Studies on Inclusive Education (**www.csie.org**) emphasises that inclusion is about rights, equity issues and social justice. It defines inclusion as:

> *Involving the processes of increasing the participation of students in, and reducing their exclusion from the cultures, curricula and communities of local schools.*

The *Index for Inclusion* (Booth et al., 2000) is possibly the most detailed explanation available about what an inclusive school 'looks like'. Here, inclusion is about creating a secure, accepting, collaborating and stimulating school in which everyone is valued and can do their best. In an inclusive school, the inclusive ethos permeates all school policies so that they increase learning and participation for all children, and school practices reflect the inclusive ethos and policies of the school (Booth et al., 2000).

Ethos and culture

Despite the lack of a commonly recognised definition, there appears to be general agreement that inclusion is related to the ethos and culture of a school and this is based on values and how people relate to, and treat, each other. Questions of school ethos, culture and belonging help us to expand the concept of inclusion and to consider diversity more broadly. Every member of school staff, through their practice, ought to aim to promote and reflect the inclusive culture and policy of the school.

As a TA, you have a responsibility and a vital role to play in promoting and supporting an inclusive 'feeling', ethos and culture. How you relate to children, in terms of teaching and learning, is crucial. Your choice of language, tone of voice and manner, for example, play a large part in establishing an ethos in which children feel safe to make mistakes and take risks with their learning. You can help to create an ethos where children feel respected and valued and where it is acceptable for children to say 'I'll try but I need some help', rather than 'I cannot do it.' Learning can only begin when we are able to say 'I do not know' (DfES, 2006), so the classroom climate needs to reflect this.

In an inclusive classroom, 'wrong' answers are not dismissed but are seen as interesting, providing an opportunity to explore the thinking that led to the answer, rather than a sign of failure. When a child gives a wrong answer, you might ask for opinions: 'That's interesting – does anyone think differently? Why?' Or you may recognise any part of the child's answer that is correct, then prompt or scaffold the same pupil to answer again rather than going on to other pupils for the 'right' answer.

An inclusive teacher or TA will let children know that, if they don't understand, that means that the adult needs to find another way of explaining; it is the adult's problem and not the child's.

When children are stuck with their work, you might say: 'Well done – if it's making you think, you are learning', or 'You've got a bit stuck – what helped you last time this happened?'

PRACTICAL TASK

Locate your school's mission statement or statement that captures its ethos and culture.

REFLECTIVE TASK

Think about the ethos and culture of your school or workplace.

- In what ways is it inclusive?
- How do you contribute towards your school's ethos?
- What can you do to help make it more inclusive?

Inclusion and special educational needs

Inclusion has frequently been associated with the education of disabled children, or of children who are categorised as SEN. This association possibly stems from outdated ideas from the 1970s and 1980s surrounding the 'integration' of children into mainstream schools.

Integration and inclusion are very different and thinking about inclusion solely in terms of school placement or where a child is educated would be a mistake. Likewise, thinking about inclusion solely in terms of SEN would be misguided. Inclusion is about the rights of *all* children and it pays attention to how the attitudes and practices of schooling can sometimes marginalise or exclude children because of their ethnicity, race, gender, ability or other factors. The quality of education of children who are categorised as having SEN or learning difficulties is part of inclusion, but it is of course by no means the whole picture.

Many TAs work in the area of SEN or learning support. The term 'special educational needs' is now increasingly regarded as an outdated term and even a discriminatory and damaging one (Corbett, 1996; Thomas and Loxley, 2001; Cole, 2005).

REFLECTIVE TASK

Why might the term 'special educational needs' be seen as discriminatory or dangerous?

Labels

The term 'special educational needs' is seen as discriminatory partly because of its association with categories, labels and stereotypes. The revised *Code of Practice* (DfES, 2001) attempted to move away from fixed categories and labels by presenting broader areas of need. Labels, however, continue to exist and place children in recognisable 'categories' of need. Although they can assist educators as a starting point for provision and can sometimes lead to additional resources and funding, labels can be problematic and damaging in that we can make wrong assumptions about learners and learners themselves can become lost behind, or even defined by, the label.

There is also a tendency for the language and practice of SEN to focus on 'remedying' or fixing 'difficulties' or 'problems', and certain practices associated with it can discriminate, segregate and exclude. Other terms that are emerging, such as 'additional needs', are regarded as more respectful, but are not, as yet, widely used in UK government policy.

Social/medical models of disability

A helpful framework for approaching understandings of inclusion, and for more fully understanding how and why the term 'special educational needs' is problematic and potentially damaging to the process of inclusion, is provided by the social and medical models of disability. Children with learning difficulties and disabilities used to be, and still are, categorised by a deficit model in that they were 'identified' as having problems or difficulty (deficit) and were subject to 'special' forms of provision. Thinking in terms of 'within-child' deficit, or lack, and categorising children in medical ways, is sometimes referred to as the medical model of disability. This model is particularly damaging for children in that it 'medicalises', or makes a problem out of, what are sometimes just differences in natural human attributes. Medical models or approaches can be subtle and wide ranging. For example, we inadvertently medicalise dyslexia by talking in terms of 'conditions' and 'diagnosis', and this is not particularly helpful to either the child with the learning needs or to the wider process of inclusion.

Medical models of thinking and of practice were very prevalent prior to moves towards greater inclusion. It is now recognised that it is more appropriate, respectful and more socially just to speak in terms of 'needs', rather than of 'difficulty' or 'conditions'. A social, rather than a medical model of disability looks to the social environment and physical spaces that can exclude or disable people; it looks to attitudes and to changing ways of thinking about, and engaging with, difference. It considers removing barriers to participation in learning.

REFLECTIVE TASK
Think about the language that you use when talking about or working with children whom you support.

- How helpful is it to talk in terms of, for example, 'children with SEN' or 'the SEN child'?
- What effect might this type of language and way of thinking have on a child's identity or sense of self?

What does this mean for a teaching assistant?

With regard to supporting teaching and learning, a social model of disability helps us to focus upon a child's needs (rather than their 'difficulties') and on adjusting features of the physical and social environment, curriculum and approaches to teaching and learning to enable those needs to be met. It means that we operate a 'can-do' philosophy and highlight children's strengths and achievements, rather than perceived limitations. Thinking about potential barriers to learning is useful as it helps us to move beyond within-child factors to consider other factors, such as the curriculum, attitudes, ethos and culture of schooling:

Inclusion is seen to involve the identification and minimising of barriers to learning and participation and the maximising of resources to support learning and participation.

(Booth et al., 2000, p13)

Some of the barriers to successful inclusion may be difficult to pin down, but they may include, for example, attitudes towards difference (Thomas and Loxley, 2001) and ways of thinking and speaking that can inadvertently cause harm, discriminate and exclude. Some particular features of schooling may also be a barrier to inclusion. For example, the way that children are grouped and how space is used in schools may have a detrimental effect on learning and participation. A widely acknowledged barrier to inclusion is the standards agenda, with its focus on national testing, academic attainment, competition and school league tables (Hall et al., 2004).

The way that you think about learners' needs and the way that you provide support for children can be crucial to successful inclusion. In the classroom, you need to develop skills and get your level of support just right, so that you can facilitate engagement, independent learning and participation.

In an inclusive classroom:
- *teachers have high expectations of all children; they are clear about the age-related expectations but also about the individual needs and differences of children in their class;*
- *children are clear about what they are learning and need to learn in order to make progress; learning objectives and success criteria are always made explicit, as are links within and between subject areas;*
- *assessment involves all the adults in the classroom and the children themselves; it is based on observation, questioning, listening and reflective responses; summative assessment is used formatively;*
- *planning takes account of a range of learning and teaching styles and offers variety and choice in method and experience for children;*
- *the reason and purpose of different access strategies are shared with both the children and other adults working in the classroom.*

(DfES, 2006)

REFLECTIVE TASK

Think about potential barriers to learning and participation in your school. How might they be addressed?

Enabling or disabling: the case of dyslexia

Inclusion requires that those who work with children are able to understand, and meet, their social, emotional and learning needs. Professional development courses can be helpful in gaining understanding of particular areas of need and of support strategies or interventions that can facilitate inclusion, but we need to be cautious about becoming 'experts' or 'specialists' in 'special educational needs' as these terms and ways of thinking (e.g. the expert knows best) can also disable a child and work against inclusion.

In light of the social model of disability, a fundamental question that we might address is: How can we develop knowledge and understanding of particular learning needs, such as dyslexia, without disabling children with that knowledge? There is no easy or straightforward answer to this question, but let us take the issue of dyslexia to demonstrate how approaches and understandings of it can enable or disable learners who are dyslexic.

Consider these case studies.

CASE STUDY 1

Peter works in a primary school and was originally employed as an in-class-support TA, but now supports pupils deemed to have particular learning needs. He is managed by the school SENCO. He was asked to attend a professional development course on specific learning difficulties in order to develop his specialism and expertise in this area. Following the course, his role has changed. He no longer works with whole classes and each week he withdraws individual children who are 'targeted' for specialist support from their lessons and he uses a diagnostic spelling programme to test, monitor and assess their progress.

In this case study we can see that the school has chosen to support the pupils by targeting them and withdrawing them for specialist support.

REFLECTIVE TASK

Looking at case study 1, what might be the benefits and drawbacks of this model of support for the pupil?

CASE STUDY 2

Tanya has been a TA for several years and has also attended a training course on specific learning needs. Tanya is careful with how she supports in that, although she has particular responsibilities for supporting a Year 6 dyslexic child called Simone (who has a statement of need), she gives her time and attention to other children in the class as well and encourages group work so that Simone is not isolated or treated very much differently from her peers. Tanya ensures that the activities that Simone engages in are in line with the teacher's lesson plans. She adapts the activities accordingly and uses multi-sensory approaches to meet Simone's particular learning needs. She finds that some of these approaches are beneficial to other children in the class.

REFLECTIVE TASK

In what ways does case study 2 differ from case study 1?

Difficulty or difference?

Dyslexia has commonly been seen as a learning difficulty, but it can just as easily be seen as a learning *difference*. If it is the school policy to view dyslexia as a learning difficulty or deficit, essentially because there is something 'wrong' with the child, then practice will tend to focus on SEN, remediation and teaching that is often carried out, as in case study 1, as something 'special' that is out of context. However, if it is the policy to view dyslexia as a learning difference, one that conveys a range of strengths and weaknesses in common with all learning styles and preferences, then practice is able to focus on inclusion, differentiation and learning (DfES, 2005).

Viewing dyslexia as a learning 'difficulty' implies that something is 'wrong' with the learner. This is reminiscent of medical models of need. It leads to a focus on identifying weaknesses rather than celebrating strengths. This, in turn, can result in an emphasis on remediation by specialists, or by 'experts', rather than resolution by knowledgeable class and subject teachers and TAs. In dyslexia-friendly schools, the focus has changed from establishing what is wrong with children in order to make them 'better', to identifying what is right in the classroom in order to enhance the effectiveness of learning.

One of the basic principles of becoming a dyslexia-friendly school is the expectation that adults in the classroom take action when faced with particular learning needs, rather than refer for assessment and wait for a 'label'. In a dyslexia-friendly school, all adults working with children are empowered, through training, policy and ethos, to recognise learning issues and take appropriate action. This is the policy of 'early intervention', which is propagated in much inclusive policy (DfES, 2003; DfES, 2004), being translated into classroom practice.

While it is acknowledged that some dyslexic learners may still require discrete specialist support at some time, the notion of dyslexia as a 'specific learning difficulty' is arguably unhelpful, certainly within the inclusive ethos of a dyslexia-friendly classroom. Your skill as a TA lies in achieving a balance between empowerment and challenge. Therefore, viewing dyslexia (or any other learning need) as a difficulty may be to misunderstand the situation. In the mainstream classroom setting, the class teacher and the TA, guided by school ethos, policy and practice, have the power to make dyslexia a learning difficulty or a learning difference.

Some examples of strategies for assisting children who carry the label 'dyslexia' are listed below. These strategies are not 'exclusive' to learners who are dyslexic and they may, of course, be of benefit to all children.

- Multi-sensory approaches. Multi-sensory teaching means using a range of ways to present information and support independent learning.
- Plan for alternatives to written recording, for example matching, sequencing, sorting, highlighting.
- ICT and the use of software.
- The use of calculators.
- Number lines and table squares.
- Writing mat templates.
- Timetable icons.
- Instructions posters.
- A 'buddy' (or TA) who can act as a scribe.
- Pair or small-group work.
- Dictionaries and thesauruses.
- Word lists.
- Key/common words.

PRACTICAL TASK

Take a look at this checklist for inclusive teaching, adapted from the Inclusive Teaching Observation Checklist for teachers (DfES, 2006), and, the next time you are supporting teaching and learning, refer to the inclusive indicators. The first box has been done for you.

Inclusive indicator	Evidence
Am I clear about what the individual or group is to learn?	Lesson notes or lesson plan.
Have I identified appropriate learning objectives?	
Is there use of multi-sensory approaches (visual, audio, kinaesthetic)?	
Is there use of interactive strategies, e.g. pupils having cards to hold up or their own whiteboards?	
Is there use of visual and tangible aids, e.g. real objects, signs or symbols, photographs, computer animations?	
Do I find ways of making abstract concepts concrete, e.g. word problems in mathematics turned into pictures or acted out or modelled with resources?	
Are tasks made more open or more closed according to pupils' needs?	
Over time, do I employ a variety of pupil groupings so that pupils are able to draw on each other's strengths and skills?	
Can all pupils see and hear me, and any resources in use (e.g. background noise avoided where possible, light source in front of me and not behind, pupils' seating carefully planned)?	
Is new or difficult vocabulary clarified, written up, displayed, returned to?	
Do I check for understanding of instructions, e.g. by asking a pupil to explain them in their own words?	
Are questions pitched so as to challenge pupils?	
Is the contribution of all learners valued – is this a secure and supportive learning environment where there is safety to have a go and make mistakes?	
Do I give time and support before responses are required, e.g. personal thinking time, partner talk, persisting with progressively more scaffolding until a pupil can answer?	
Do I promote independence, protect self-esteem and increase pupils' inclusion within their peer group?	

Inclusive indicator	Evidence
Are tasks clearly explained or modelled – checks for understanding, task cards or boards as reminders, time available and expected outcomes made clear?	
Are pupils provided with, and regularly reminded of, resources to help them be independent?	
Is scaffolding used (e.g. problem-solving grids, talk and writing frames, clue cards) to support learners?	
Have I made arrangements where necessary to ensure that all children can access written text or instructions?	
Have I planned alternatives to paper-and-pencil tasks, where appropriate?	
Does the teacher make effective use of ICT as an access strategy (e.g. speech-supported or sign-supported software, on-screen word banks, predictive word processing)?	
Is appropriate behaviour noticed and praised or rewarded?	
Are learners involved in setting their own targets and monitoring their own progress?	

CHAPTER SUMMARY

- Inclusion is a concept and a process that involves change. TAs can assist the process of inclusion and enhance inclusive school cultures.
- Inclusion is about all children. The phrase 'special educational needs' needs to be used cautiously with reference to inclusion.
- Ethos, attitudes and culture can influence the effectiveness of inclusion.

REFERENCES

Booth, T., Ainscow, M., Black-Hawkins, K., Vaughan, M. and Shaw, L. (2002) *Index for Inclusion.* Bristol: Centre for Studies in Inclusive Education.

Cole, B.A. (2005) Mission impossible? Special educational needs, inclusion and the re-conceptualization of the role of the SENCO in England and Wales. *European Journal of Special Needs Education,* 20(3): 287–307.

Corbett, J. (1996) *Bad-Mouthing: The language of special needs.* London: The Falmer Press.

Department for Education and Employment (DfEE) (1997) *Excellence for All Children: Meeting special educational needs.* London: DfEE.

Department for Education and Employment (DfEE) (1998) *Meeting Special Educational Needs: A programme of action.* London: DfEE.

Department for Education and Employment (DfEE) (1999) *Curriculum 2000*. London: DfEE.

Department for Education and Skills (DfES) (2001) *Revised Code of Practice on the Identification and Assessment of Special Educational Needs*. London: DfES.

Department for Education and Skills (DfES) (2003) *Every Child Matters: Green paper on children's services*. Norwich: TSO.

Department for Education and Skills (DfES) (2004) *Removing Barriers to Achievement: The government's strategy for SEN*. London: DfES.

Department for Education and Skills (DfES) (2005) *Learning and Teaching for Dyslexic Children (Primary National Strategy)*. London: DfES.

Department for Education and Skills (DfES) (2006) *Leading on Intervention*. London: DfES.

Department for Education and Skills (DfES) (2007) *Inclusion Development Programme*. London: DfES.

Hall, K., Collins, J., Benjamin, S., Nind, M. and Sheehy, K. (2004) SATurated models of pupildom: assessment and inclusion/exclusion. *British Educational Research Journal*, 30(6): 801–17.

HM Government (2001) *Special Educational Needs and Disability Act*. London: HMSO.

OFSTED (2001) Evaluating Educational Inclusion HMI 235 (e-publication). Available online at www.ofsted.gov.uk/publications.

Richards, G. and Armstrong, F. (2008) *Key Issues for Teaching Assistants: Working in diverse and inclusive classrooms*. London: RoutledgeFalmer.

Sorsby, C. (2004) Forging and strengthening alliances: learning support staff and the challenge of inclusion, in F. Armstrong and M. Moore (eds) *Action Research for Inclusive Education: Changing places, changing practices, changing minds*. London: RoutledgeFalmer.

Thomas, G. and Loxley, A. (2001) *Deconstructing Special Education and Constructing Inclusion*. Buckingham: Open University Press.

UNESCO (1994) *The Salamanca Statement and Framework for Action on Special Needs Education. World Conference on Special Needs Education, Access and Quality*. Available online at www.unesco.org/education/educpro/sne/salamanc/index.htm (accessed 13 September 2008).

WEBSITES

http://inclusion.ngfl.gov.uk/
www.csie.org.uk   The Centre for Studies on Inclusive Education (CSIE)
www.dyslexiaaction.org.uk   Dyslexia-friendly classrooms
www.standards.dfes.gov.uk   The Standards site

FURTHER READING

Richards, G. and Armstrong, F. (2008) *Key Issues for Teaching Assistants: Working in diverse and inclusive classrooms*. London: RoutledgeFalmer.

6 BEHAVIOUR FOR LEARNING

Alexis Moore and Joanne Sutcliffe

CHAPTER OBJECTIVES

By the end of this chapter you will:

- gain an understanding of developmental stages of behaviour;
- understand the importance of behaviour for learning and 'learning behaviour';
- identify strategies to enable you to promote positive behaviour;
- start to develop an understanding of moderate and specific learning difficulties.

LINKS TO **HLTA** STANDARDS

1. Demonstrate the positive values, attitudes and behaviour they expect from children and young people.

2. Understand the key factors that affect children's and young people's learning and progress.

3 Use effective strategies to promote positive behaviour.

These standards cannot be viewed in isolation as each one is inter-related. Consistently modelling the types of behaviours expected of the children that you work with will contribute to a positive learning environment and enable children to develop positive learning behaviours.

Introduction

Over the past 50 years, the school approach to behaviour has evolved from one that is mainly based on sanctions and punishment to one that is based on positive reinforcement and support. The role of the teaching assistant (TA) in supporting behaviour for learning is very important and one that is often underestimated.

The government commissioned a report published in 1989, *The Elton Report: Enquiry into discipline in schools* (HM Government, 1989). This report forms the basis of many current guidance documents, policies and legislation in schools and settings today. The report suggested that schools should 'plan' to manage behaviour in a positive rather than a reactive way. This report also established the link between classroom management, organisation and the curriculum and found that the quality of teaching and learning has a 'significant' impact on behaviour. In 1989, when the report was written, there were very few adults working in classrooms who were not teachers, and the significant impact of the TA within the school could not have been anticipated.

Following this, in 2005, a review was commissioned by the DfES and chaired by Sir Alan Steer that resulted in *The Report of The Practitioners' Group on School Behaviour and Discipline* (DfES, 2005a). The report was based on a set of six core beliefs.

- *The quality of learning, teaching and behaviour in schools [comprises] inseparable issues, and [is] the responsibility of all staff.*
- *Poor behaviour cannot be tolerated, as it is a denial of the right of the pupils to learn and teachers to teach. To enable learning to take place, preventative action is the most effective, but where this fails, schools must have clear, firm and intelligent strategies in place to help pupils manage their behaviour.*
- *There is no single solution to the problem of poor behaviour, but all schools have the potential to raise standards if they are consistent in implementing good practice in learning, teaching and behaviour management.*
- *Respect has to be given in order to be received. Parents and carers, pupils and teachers all need to operate in a culture of mutual regard.*
- *The support of parents is essential for the maintenance of good behaviour. Parents and schools each need to have a clear understanding of their rights and responsibilities.*
- *School leaders have a critical role in establishing high standards of learning, teaching and behaviour.*

(DfES, 2005a)

Following this report there have been a number of initiatives to enable schools and settings to promote positive behaviour for learning. The behaviour strands of the primary and secondary national strategies in the social and emotional aspects of learning, also known as the SEAL programme (DfES, 2005b), have been adopted by many schools. New roles within schools have emerged in order to support learning and behaviour in the form of learning mentors, behaviour and attendance officers and lead behaviour specialists (NPSLBA – National Programme for Specialist Leaders of Behaviour and Attendance). There are also behaviour improvement programmes (BIPs), and other roles are continuing to emerge, such as the family support assistant (FSA).

Models for behaviour management have been based on behaviourist theories, such as those of Skinner, Pavlov and Thorndyke. Behaviourist theorists suggest that all behaviour is learned and is subject to conditioning. Consequently, desired behaviours can be encouraged by reward and undesired behaviours can be discouraged by punishment. Other theorists suggest that behaviour is dependent on social conditions and how individuals interact. For more information regarding theories relating to behaviour and learning, see Watkinson (2003), Hryniewicz (2004) and Bentham (2006).

PRACTICAL TASK
Obtain a copy of policy relating to behaviour in school.

- Identify language relating to positive aspects of behaviour.
- Identify agreed rewards and sanctions.

- Do you follow the agreed systems?
- How do you model positive behaviour for learning in school?
- What do you see your responsibility to be in promoting positive behaviours for learning?

Understanding behaviour

All learning behaviour is rooted in relationships and positive relationships facilitate learning .
EPPI-centre, 2004, p82

Following the EPPI-centre review of how learning theories explain behaviour in school contexts, the team of reviewers held the view that the 'fostering of learning behaviour' or 'behaviour for learning' was the foundation of effective behaviour management rather than 'learning to behave'.

The diagram in Figure 6.1 is adapted from the EPPI-centre review. The suggestion is that all learning behaviour is dependent upon relationships. The relationship that the learner has with learning and the consequential self-image as a learner; the relationship the learner has with the curriculum and its relevance to them personally; and the relationship the learner has with others, including peers and adults. While a pupil's learning behaviour is influenced by relationships, in turn these relationships are influenced by other factors, such as family, policy and other agencies.

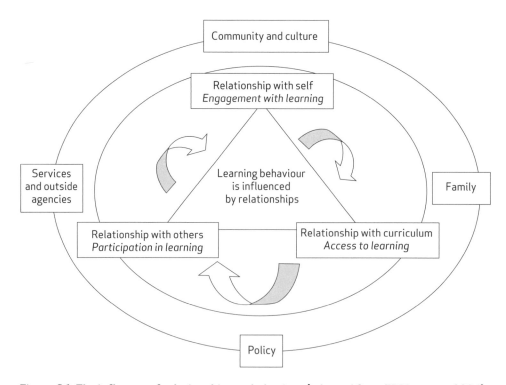

Figure 6.1: The influence of relationships on behaviour (adapted from EPPI-centre, 2004)

While, for the majority of children, the balance between these factors means that children develop good behaviours for learning, there are undoubtedly groups of vulnerable children for whom the balance changes. As such, we as educators need to be aware of any external influences affecting an individual's 'learning behaviour' and of the past experiences and perceptions the child may have. In this way the holistic learning needs of pupils can be addressed.

Developmental stages in learning behaviours

Learning to behave in a socially acceptable manner is something that is usually recognised as having 'milestones' linked to social development. One would not expect a teenager to respond to being told they could not go and play in the garden in the same way as a two year old, although some parents of teenagers may disagree.

The *Statutory Framework for the Early Years Foundation Stage* (EYFS) (DCSF, 2008) has four themes that express key principles underpinning effective practice in EYFS.

1. A Unique Child – every child is a competent learner who can be resilient, capable, confident and self-assured.
2. Positive Relationships – children learn to be strong and independent from a base of loving and secure relationships with parents and/or a key person.
3. Enabling Environments – the environment plays a key role in supporting and extending children's development and learning.
4. Learning and Development – children develop and learn in different ways and at different rates and all areas of learning and development are equally important and interconnected.

From this, it may be assumed that learning behaviours are embedded across the curriculum and throughout the Early Years' settings (ibid.).

A new baby learns to expect responses to certain behaviours very quickly as its social development skills start to develop. The impact of modelled behaviours from adults and peers is crucial to development (ibid.).

By nursery and reception age, children build a stronger identity of self and their place in the world. They start to recognise the importance of social rules and customs; they develop understanding and tolerance, and learn how to be more controlled in their own behaviour. Social skills are further developed when playing in small groups; there is a developing understanding of sensitivity to the needs, views and feelings of others and of cause, effect and consequences. Children understand what is right and wrong and why. At this stage children express needs and feelings in appropriate ways (ibid.).

When children have difficulties in their lives or face adversity, it may be that some of these stages are not fully developed. When dealing with behaviours that are not age appropriate, it can be useful to think of these stages and how you would respond if the pupil were a younger child. In these cases, children need some guidance as to the appropriate responses when they are calm, for example 'I know you are angry but when you are screaming and shouting, it is difficult to understand what you are angry about. When you are calm, you can tell me and we can find a solution.'

Challenging behaviours

Nutbrown and Clough (2006, p28) suggest that challenging behaviours in the Early Years are defined by the environment in which the behaviours take place. So in an Early Years environment children are encouraged to access the outdoors, go to use the bathroom when it is needed, make choices for independent learning during the session, and communicate ideas with their peers and adults at most times of the day. These types of behaviour are clearly not acceptable in the more formal setting of Year 6 and, if they were displayed, may be described as 'challenging'. Acceptable behaviours relate to the development of social skills and relationships.

Just as current initiatives in education suggest that identifying the 'What's in it for me?' (WIIFM) aspects of learning for pupils will increase motivation, this can be a useful analogy for educators to think about when presented with challenging behaviours. Watkinson describes behaviours displayed by pupils as *fulfilling a need* (2003, p114); the skill in understanding behaviours is what motivates a pupil to behave in a particular way. The pupil may behave in a particular way in order to provoke a reaction or response, which is the WIIFM factor. Watkinson describes these behaviours as relating to attention, affection, protection or power. Consequently, considering the reasons why a child is behaving in a particular way can help with your response. This is a key element in developing an understanding of behaviour. For example, the child who needs attention will not necessarily be able to distinguish between 'positive' and 'negative' attention; either way they will have one-to-one interactions with the adult.

A key aspect to managing behaviour is to develop a proactive approach that plans for positive behaviour, rather than always having to adopt a reactive response to both positive and negative behaviours. When you *react* to behaviour it can often be an instinctive response, but this is sometimes necessary. For example, if there is a dangerous situation that you see about to happen, you may shout 'STOP!' to avoid that potential danger. However, it would be hoped that this would then be followed by an explanation of why you raised your voice and what the possible consequences could have been of the dangerous behaviour.

> ### REFLECTIVE TASK
> If you were a person who constantly raised your voice within the classroom, what do you think would happen if you shouted 'STOP'? Would there be any significant reaction from the pupils?

Learning environment

There are many aspects to creating a learning environment that incorporate planning for positive behaviours. The establishment of routines, rules and rituals can provide security for pupils when linked to rights and responsibilities. Rogers (2007, p126) suggests that a key factor of behaviour management is the language we use and consideration of the following principles.

- Educators must be confident in dealing with behaviours and be aware of both verbal and non-verbal communications. What do you think your body language would convey to pupils if you were standing with your arms folded and your foot tapping?

- A calm, controlled approach should be adopted and you should ensure that you are calm before trying to calm a pupil.
- Language should focus on the behaviour rather than be a verbal attack on the individual.
- Instructions, requests and commands should be brief and focus on behaviour.
- Pupils need to be given enough 'take-up time' when possible to comply with instructions, even if this means ignoring some secondary behaviours in the meantime.
- Ensure that correcting behaviours is balanced with encouragement and there is an expectation that working relationships will be re-established.
- Concentrate and focus on the 'primary behaviours' and 'primary issues' relating to rules, responsibilities and rights rather than being distracted by the secondary behaviours that may be displayed by pupils, such as sighing, shrugging shoulders, having to have the last word, etc.
- Make sure that you are consistent in your approach, having an agreed level of sanctions and rewards.
- In line with school policy, involve other people, other adults within school and parents for both positive and negative aspects of behaviour.
- Maintain the respect and dignity of pupils by using the least intrusive approach; this can avoid situations escalating and can work within the agreed level of responses, rewards and sanctions.
- Provide support for pupils to make reparation and reconciliation in order that this becomes a recognised part of the process.

As adults within the school setting, it can be argued that it is our responsibility to model the desired behaviours. If we expect a calm, consistent environment with clarity about what is, and is not, acceptable behaviour within that environment, then we have to demonstrate that we too follow this code. For many children and young people within our care, their school or setting may be one of the few environments that consistently display these values.

CASE STUDY 1

Scenario 1

In Class A, the children come into school, hang up their coats, take their reading book bags into the classroom and put them in their trays. Some children get activities out and start to play; others sit on the carpet waiting for the teacher. When the teacher comes to the carpet to take the register, she tells the children doing activities to put them away. In doing so, they put away the activities that are on the table ready for the next session. The TA is getting the book bags from the trays and is changing the books for the children. There is a pile of bags she cannot deal with as there are queries about the next book. Charlie is engrossed in making a tower and, in an effort to get him to come to the carpet for register, his friend starts to dismantle the tower. Charlie shouts at him to stop and then hits him and both children are now crying. The teacher leaves the carpet to deal with the disagreement. The TA starts to take the register. The activities that children are sent to are incomplete and children are not on task.

Scenario 2

In Class B, the Foundation Stage practitioner has developed a self-registration system for the mornings. Children find their name and photograph card on a table and 'velcro' it to the register list displayed at child height on the wall. They put their book bag in a labelled box and the TA talks to them about the books they have read. There is a number of activities out on the tables that children can access freely. Some of these activities have a cartoon alligator placed on top. The children know this is a signal that this equipment is not to be played with before the first carpet time of the morning. There is a number of cartoon alligators available for children to use if they are in the middle of a model when it is time to tidy up for the first session. This avoids upset and allows children to sustain concentration. Children are given a 'five-minute' cue time for coming to the carpet, which allows them to tidy their area, put pictures away and put alligators on tasks that they want to keep; it also encourages collaboration and helping each others. Children are ready on the carpet for the teaching input, which starts with a 'Well done' for coming into the classroom sensibly and a short discussion about choosing activities.

REFLECTIVE TASK

Which classroom, in case study 1, would you rather be in if you were five years old? Why? What can you do to make your classroom a supportive environment that encourages behaviour for learning?

A key factor in behaviour for learning is planning for positive behaviour outcomes. As can be seen from the examples in case study 1, the responsibility is on the adults within schools and settings to create a learning environment in which pupils are safe and secure. Pupils should be given opportunities to develop independence and scaffolds within which they can make choices and develop positive attitudes to learning. In this way children can 'learn' acceptable behaviours.

Creating routines and rituals within the classroom will enable children to know they are 'doing the right thing'. Positive re-enforcement of this behaviour by adults and peers encourages these behaviours to be perpetuated and frees time for adults to deal with the important issues of developing positive relationships and learning rather than reacting to and dealing with behavioural incidents. This is particularly important for pupils who display challenging behaviours. By providing a predictable, positive learning environment, children are more likely to be able to conform rather than having to 'guess' what the teacher/practitioner wants.

Moderate learning difficulties and the impact on behaviour for learning

There is a range of differing perspectives on the terminology used to describe learning difficulties and additional needs. The DfES describes the category of children who have moderate learning difficulties:

[Pupils with MLD] will have attainments significantly below expected levels in most areas of the curriculum, despite appropriate interventions [and their needs will not be met by] normal differentiation and the flexibilities of the National Curriculum. [They] have much greater difficulty than peers in acquiring basic literacy and numeracy skills and in understanding

*concepts [and may experience] speech and language delay, low self-esteem, low levels of
concentration and underdeveloped social skills.*

(DfES, 2005b, p3)

Pupils who have moderate learning difficulties (MLD), sometimes referred to as 'global learning difficulties', usually have a statement of SEN or will be included on the school or setting's special needs/inclusion register at 'School Action Plus'. This group of children comprises the majority of children on the SEN register in mainstream schools.

For these children, there are often associated difficulties in accessing the curriculum in terms of relevance, developing relationships with peers and maintaining a positive self-image as a learner. The triangle of relationships affecting behaviour in Figure 6.1 (see page 68) is particularly pertinent for children with significant learning needs. Children with any additional learning needs, and particularly children who have speech and language delay, may need alternative strategies in order to assist them in developing a positive self-image and making good choices with behaviour.

There is a number or strategies that can be used to avoid conflict and encourage independence. These may include using picture cues to describe the desired behaviours, using picture cues to give structure and order to the day, following routines and rituals and encouraging children to predict what is going to happen next so that they develop personal independence. Often, limited choice can be accompanied by a physical cue. For example, a TA may hold out two hands: (holding out the right hand) 'Do you want to tidy up your work space by yourself?' or (holding out the left hand) 'Would you like me to help you?' The child can then touch the hand to indicate the choice.

By creating a positive learning environment, potential difficulties with behaviour for learning can be avoided. To support more challenging behaviour the following strategies may be useful.

- Use scale pictures from 1–10 to help children describe how they are feeling, particularly when angry.
- Teach techniques for reducing stress, anger and anxiety.
- Reinforce positive messages regarding behaviour, e.g. 'Well done for letting Simon be first in the line', 'You were very patient when you let Harry use the pencil sharpener first.' Also make observations regarding other children's behaviours, e.g. 'Harry was very kind when he asked you to play tag with him.'
- Role play social situations that can cause conflict or upset to rehearse responses, e.g. 'If you do not want to play say, No thank you.'
- Give clear, limited options and choices for behaviour.
- Be consistent; understand choices for behaviour, but the agreed consequences of the choice should still stand.
- Find solutions rather than focus on problems, and encourage children to think through actions and reparation, e.g. 'How can you make things better after you pushed Simon out of the line?'

Specific learning difficulties and the impact on behaviour for learning

With specific learning difficulties (SpLD), we examine the concern that, if strategies are not developed to enhance learning, behavioural difficulties may arise. There are conflicting perspectives concerning the terminology used to describe learning and behavioural difficulties. Currently, the DCSF uses the definitions described earlier in this chapter. The debate on the labelling of special, specific, moderate and additional educational needs is further discussed in the chapter on inclusion (Chapter 5). Teachernet offers the following description of the spectrum of SpLD:

Specific learning difficulties is an umbrella term which indicates that pupils display differences across their learning. Pupils with SpLD may have a particular difficulty in learning to read, write, spell or manipulate numbers so that their performance in these areas is below their performance in other areas. Pupils may also have problems with short-term memory, organisational skills and co-ordination. Pupils with SpLD cover the whole ability range and the severity of their impairment varies widely.

(teachernet, 2008)

The SpLDs discussed within this chapter are:

- dyslexia;
- dyscalculia;
- dyspraxia.

Learning difficulties that could lead to behavioural difficulties

Pupils with dyslexia, dyscalculia and dyspraxia may never display behavioural difficulties or problems. However, it is important to understand that these can arise and can lead to significant behavioural issues if they are not managed carefully. Students can become frustrated and annoyed, which may discourage them from learning and may lead others to become unable to learn.

Dyslexia

Dyslexia is an SpLD that impedes the learning of literacy skills, that is, a dyslexic person has problems learning to read, write and spell. This problem with managing verbal codes in memory is neurologically based and tends to run in families (Hryniewicz, 2004). Other symbolic systems, such as mathematics and reading music, can also be affected. Dyslexia can occur at any level of intellectual ability. It can accompany, but is not a result of, lack of motivation, emotional disturbance and/or sensory impairment. An individual is identified as dyslexic when a significant discrepancy exists between intellectual ability and reading performance without an apparent alternative cause.

The following suggestions may help deal with aspects of this difficulty to ensure that we promote positive behaviour for learning.

- Provide multi-sensory teaching and structured learning, always building upon prior learning.
- Ensure plenty of practice is provided in relation to areas of work and slowly build up the development of these areas, which may lead to giving smaller, more manageable tasks. Ensure that all instructions are short and clear.
- Allow extra time for answering questions as pupils may need to integrate and combine various subjects.
- When producing work, use large fonts, relevant coloured paper and mind maps and utilise look, say, write, cover, check.

Dyscalculia

Dyscalculia is defined by Sousa as a condition that leaves individuals with *a difficulty in conceptualising numbers, number relationships, outcomes of numerical operations, and estimation* (2007, p143). This could include a difficulty in acquiring simple number concepts, an inability to grasp innate number facts and procedures and no confidence in the answers or methods they choose, even if correct. Pupils will have an impaired sense of number size, will have difficulties comparing numbers and will have problems with estimating numbers in a collection. It is clear that, if pupils struggle with mathematics, behavioural problems can arise, as often specific, correct answers are needed that they are unable to provide; and an anxiety about mathematics leads to problems, for example pupils wanting to avoid the subject at all costs.

The following suggestions may help deal with aspects of this difficulty to ensure that we promote positive behaviour for learning.

- Keep worksheets uncluttered and well spaced out and, wherever possible, include clear steps and instructions. Keep any worksheet as multi-sensory as possible.
- Ensure that the student is aware of the mathematical concept, as many will learn sequences by rote and then find it impossible to use these when not in the specific order they have learned. Pupils with dyscalculia will also have problems making their own sequencing instructions, so plenty of support is needed.
- Use as many visual aids as possible, as most pupils will have a poor sense of direction, will have difficulty in telling the time and will find it hard to handle money. This means providing lots of real-life experiences linked to these mathematical activities and, wherever possible, using repetition.

Dyspraxia

Dyspraxia is when messages are not properly transmitted to the body due to an immaturity in the brain that causes problems with motor co-ordination (Brownhill, 2007). Dyspraxia is a disability, but is not apparent to others, which can be both an advantage and a disadvantage to the individual. Aspects of dyspraxia may be interpreted as behavioural problems, but are in fact characteristics of it. This may include younger children becoming aggressive due to lack of communication skills, thereby having difficulty establishing friendships. This could lead to the impression that the pupil is a loner and an introvert. It is often difficult to reason with a pupil with dyspraxia, and temper tantrums can be common. Other difficulties include speech problems and difficulty answering questions, although answers are known. This could result in the pupil being seen as unco-operative. Pupils may have reading and writing difficulties and an inability to hold a pen or pencil correctly, although this may not be a problem on other occasions.

Although there is no cure for dyspraxia, specialist help can promote a greater chance of improvement.

- Occupational therapists and physiotherapists can help the individual overcome many difficulties, although many skills we take for granted will never become automatic for a dyspraxic child.
- Extra help in school will help teach these skills, which can then help with overcoming other difficulties.
- If content is the more desired outcome for a lesson and presentation is less important, it is essential that collaboration including full support is given with writing, drawing and the plan of work.

Aspects of social, emotional and behavioural difficulties that could have an effect upon learning

Attention deficit disorders

Attention deficit disorder (ADD) and attention deficit hyperactivity disorder (ADHD) can affect children at all stages of education and are more common in boys. Pupils with ADD/ADHD often suffer from dyspraxia as well. If pupils with ADD/ADHD are not offered specific support in relation to their learning, this could severely impair their development and opportunities for learning. A lack of support could also lead to behavioural problems, which could then have an effect upon the learning of others within that educational environment. Aspects of ADD/ADHD that may be misinterpreted as behavioural problems can include struggling to follow instructions and complete set tasks, being easily distracted and forgetful and having difficulty listening when spoken to. Pupils with ADD/ADHD often fidget, squirm and can't sit still. They may also be unable to stop talking and, annoyingly, will constantly interrupt others. The pupils may also blurt out answers without waiting to be asked, as they have difficulty awaiting their turn and will act impulsively without thinking about consequences.

It is extremely important to initially pinpoint the difficulties an individual may be experiencing, as support time can be wasted and the individual can feel frustrated if support is given in an area where few difficulties emerge (Sousa, 2007). Other suggestions to help deal with this difficulty include the following.

- Keep timetables and lessons as predictable as possible by creating a daily routine.
- Set short achievable tasks and be very specific with any instructions for tasks.
- Give immediate rewards, including praise and attention when behaviour is good, and make clear reasonable requests for behaviour.
- Keep rules simple and clear, set boundaries that are easily understood and ensure consistency in managing the pupil. This includes the use of rewards and sanctions.

- Plan learning to gradually lengthen the pupil's concentration and ability to focus on tasks.
- It is important to communicate with the pupil on a one-to-one basis and ensure that this is not interrupted by others.

Autistic spectrum disorder

Autistic spectrum disorder (ASD) includes autism and Asperger's syndrome. Autism is a life-long developmental disability that prevents individuals from properly understanding what they see, hear and otherwise sense, which can result in severe problems with social relationships, communication and behaviour. Autistic children will have severe delay in language development and in understanding social relationships. They will have inconsistent patterns of sensory responses and uneven patterns of intellectual functioning. Autistic children will also show a marked restriction in activities and interests. Asperger's syndrome is characterised by severe and sustained impairment in social interaction, and the development of restricted and repetitive patterns of behaviour, interests and activities (Sousa, 2007). Pupils with Asperger's will often be unaware of others' feelings, so are unable to carry on with a 'give and take' conversation. This can lead to an inability to develop peer relationships that are appropriate to the developmental level. Any changes in routines and transition can cause upset.

It is important to remember that any misbehaviour is not personal and the following suggestions can help deal with this difficulty.

- Ensure that the individual is organised for their learning, which can include breaking things down into smaller steps.
- Be as concrete as possible and be aware of literal speech. This may be avoiding excess verbal communication.
- Reduce stress by decreasing unusual or difficult behaviours and keep any changes to routine minimal.
- Facial expressions (or other social cues) may not work with children who lie within the autistic spectrum.

Conduct disorder

Conduct disorder (CD) refers to a group of behavioural and emotional problems in which individuals act towards others in a destructive way (Sousa, 2007). Individuals with this disorder have great difficulty following rules and behaving in a socially acceptable way. Behavioural issues include showing aggression towards people and animals, including bullying, threatening and intimidation. There is a deliberate destruction of property and sufferers will steal, as long as there is no confrontation. A pupil will also show signs of deceitfulness and lying and will display serious violations of rules, both at home and school.

Specialist help is needed to deal with this disorder.

- Comprehensive and specific help is often needed, which may have to take place in different settings.
- Behaviour therapy and psychotherapy are often needed to help with this disorder. Treatment is a longer-term process, as in most cases patterns of behaviour and attitude need to be altered.

Oppositional defiance disorder

Oppositional defiance disorder (ODD) is constant disobedience and an opposition to various authoritative persons, including *parents, teachers and other adults* (Sousa, 2007, p168). However, the basic rights of others are respected and age-appropriate rules are not violated. This disorder displays several behavioural problems, which can include frequent temper tantrums. Pupils with ODD may also have unnecessary and sometimes extreme arguments with adults and these may come from an active defiance and refusal to comply with adult requests. The pupils will upset and annoy people deliberately; however, they will also be easily annoyed by others. They may also be quick-tempered and become easily upset, and will show frequent anger and resentment towards others, which often leads to revenge seeking. There will also be no responsibility taken for their mistakes or misbehaviour.

There are various suggestions to help deal with this disorder.

- A behavioural modification programme is needed, which can be developed in the classroom. This may involve:
  - ensuring behaviour to be observed is clearly specified in terms of 'actions and performance';
  - establishing a 'baseline' so that any modification in behaviour can be measured;
  - setting goals that encourage academic and social development;
  - determining signals and prompts that help direct individuals to behave in a particular manner;
  - determining positive reinforcements for appropriate behaviour and, when necessary, punishments, which can only stop bad behaviours, not promote desirable ones;
  - evaluating the behavioural modification programme to determine success and ways forward.
- It is important to give a lot of praise and encouragement when the pupil is co-operative and working well. This may be for small areas of improvement in the first instance; however, these could be huge steps for the pupil. For example, praise for sitting down when asked may seem pointless to others, but could be very important for the pupil. It important to note also that this doesn't have to be done in front of the whole class.
- There is little point in arguing with the pupil. It is more important to show them that there will not be any confrontational engagement, even if this means removal of the pupil or the rest of the group (as the learning needs of others have to be met). The situation is easier to deal with when there is a calm environment and then discussions can take place linked to the behaviour modification programme.

Obsessive compulsive disorder

Obsessive compulsive disorder (OCD) is an anxiety disorder in which a person has unreasonable thoughts, fears or worries and tries to manage this by performing ritual activities in the hope that these reduce the anxiety. Sousa indicates that *This disorder involves patterns of repeated thoughts and behaviours that are impossible to control or to stop* (2007, p165). Areas include an extreme preoccupation with dirt, germs or contamination and obtrusive thoughts about violence, hurting, killing someone or self-harming. Other compulsive behaviours include checking and rechecking, following rigid rules of order and hoarding objects, as well as the repetition of words, questions, obscenities, obscene actions, sounds and music. Specialist help such as behaviour therapy and medication is normally required, and a combination of both is usually most effective.

The suggestions given in this chapter can only ever be a guide to strategies that could be adopted in order to support children in behaviour for learning and learning behaviours. Each school will have individual approaches within a national framework for behaviour and each child will have individual needs, some of which will need a more personalised response.

The key to developing positive behaviours is relationships based on mutual respect and harnessing motivation to learn. For some children, this is linked to developmental stages and social and emotional needs that have to be addressed alongside learning. However, for all children, we would want them to develop self-management strategies and independence. Behaviour for learning is an intrinsic part of school, the curriculum and each person within the school community:

> *Central to the development of learning behaviour is motivation and self-discipline to move students from externally driven strategies toward the self-motivation and self-regulation needed for life-long learning and achievement.*

(EPPI-centre, 2004, p88)

CHAPTER SUMMARY

- The quality of learning, teaching and behaviour in schools comprises inseparable issues, and is the responsibility of all staff.
- Behaviour is learned and children go through developmental stages. These may not always be age appropriate, so children need support with their behaviour.
- Behaviour for learning and learning to behave are interrelated. It is the role of educators to enable children to develop skills and understanding about positive behaviour choices.
- There is a range of strategies and approaches that can be personalised within an agreed school system to meet individual learning and behavioural needs.

REFERENCES

Bentham, S. (2006) *A Teaching Assistant's Guide to Managing Behaviour in the Classroom*. Abingdon: Routledge.

Brownhill, S. (2007) *Taking the Stress out of Bad Behaviour*. London: Continuum.

Department for Children, Schools and Families (DCSF) (2008) *Statutory Framework for the Early Years Foundation Stage May 2008*. Nottingham: DCSF Publications.

Department for Education and Skills (DfES) (2005a) *The Report of The Practitioners' Group on School Behaviour and Discipline*. London: DfES.

Department for Education and Skills (DfES) (2005b) *Excellence and Enjoyment: Social and emotional aspects of learning*. London: DfES. Available online at www.standards.dfes.gov.uk (ref. DfES 1378–2005G) (accessed 16 October 2008).

EPPI-centre (2004) *A Systematic Review of How Theories Explain Learning Behaviour in School Contexts*. Available online at eppi.ioe.ac.uk (accessed 16 October 2008).

HM Government (1989) *The Elton Report: Enquiry into discipline in schools*. London: HMSO.

Hryniewicz, L. (2004) *Teaching Assistants: The Complete Handbook*. Cambridge: Adamson Publishing.

Nutbrown, C. and Clough, P. (2006) *Inclusion in the Early Years*. London: Sage.

Rogers, B. (2007) *Behaviour Management: A whole school approach* (2nd edn). London: Paul Chapman.

Sousa, D.A. (2007) *How the Special Needs Brain Learns* (2nd edn). London: Sage.

teachernet (2008) *Cognition and Learning Needs*. Available online at www.teachernet.gov.uk/wholeschool/sen/datatypes/cognitionlearningneeds/(accessed 4 November 2008).

Watkinson, A. (2003) *The Essential Guide for Experienced Teaching Assistants*. London: David Fulton Publishers.

FURTHER reading

Adams, K. (2009) *Behaviour for Learning in the Primary School: Achieving QTS*. Exeter: Learning Matters.

Imray, P. (2007) *Turning the Tables on Challenging Behaviour: A practitioner's perspective to transforming challenging behaviours in children, young people and adults with SLD, PMD or ASD*. London: Taylor and Francis.

Rogers, B. (2004) *How to Manage Children's Challenging Behaviour*. London: Paul Chapman.

Rogers, B. and McPherson, E. (208) *Behaviour Management with Young Children: Crucial first steps with children 3–7 years*. London: Paul Chapman.

WEBSITE

www.behaviour4learning.ac.uk

PART 2

SUPPORTING INNOVATION AND CHANGE

7 TEACHING AND LEARNING

Susan Faragher

CHAPTER OBJECTIVES

By the end of this chapter you will:

- understand the developmental, social constructivist and behaviourist approaches underpinning how children learn;
- understand the role learning styles and multiple intelligences play in pupils' learning;
- understand the importance of a positive learning climate on motivation and learning.

LINKS TO **HLTA** STANDARDS

1. Understand the key factors that affect children's and young people's learning and progress.
2. Know how to contribute to effective personalised provision by taking practical account of diversity.
3. Understand the objectives, content and intended outcomes for learning activities in which they are involved.
4. Devise clearly structured activities that interest and motivate learners and advance their learning.
5. Advance learning when working with individuals.
6. Advance learning when working with small groups.
7. Advance learning when working with whole classes without the presence of the assigned teacher.

Introduction

In this chapter you will reflect on the theories underpinning how children learn, including developmental, social constructivist and behaviourist approaches, relating this to your own practice. Through an explanation of learning styles and multiple intelligences you will consider how knowledge of these can promote children's learning and you will reflect on the importance of a positive learning climate in promoting children's motivation and learning.

Theories of how children learn

In the late nineteenth and early twentieth centuries, educational scientists equated mental ability with the ability to learn and ultimately a measure of intelligence. Alfred Binet (1857–1911) was a law graduate who became fascinated with psychology and is most widely known for his work on intelligence:

> It seems to us that in intelligence there is a fundamental faculty, the alteration or the lack of which, is of the utmost importance for practical life. This faculty is judgement . . . A person may be a moron or an imbecile if he is lacking in judgment . . . Indeed the rest of intellectual faculties seem of little importance in comparison to judgement.
>
> (Binet and Simon, 1916/1973, pp42–3)

Binet had two daughters whom he researched initially to refine his view of intelligence. He was joined in his work in 1920 by Théodore Simon and together they created what is known as the Binet–Simon scale. This comprised a set of tasks that they believed, through intensive research, were typical of children's abilities at certain ages. Their aim was to be able to compare children's mental abilities with those of their peers. There was a 30-point scale of increasing difficulty and the score achieved was deemed to be the child's mental age. This, they believed, was intrinsically linked to the ability to learn.

Binet and Simon were fully aware of the limitations of their tests and did not intend to create a *scale of intelligence* (Entwistle, 1996, p141). However, the tasks scale soon became used in this way and was further developed into the formulation of an intelligence quotient (IQ).

Since this time, there has been a succession of educational theorists searching for the way in which children learn. They basically fall into two broad categories – behaviourists and constructivists.

Behaviourists believe that learning is the acquisition of any new behaviour that relies totally on the observation of this behaviour. The two types are:

- classic conditioning, which is a natural reflex action to a stimulus; Pavlov showed an example of this when he trained dogs to salivate on a signal that food was about to be brought to them;
- behavioural conditioning, when a response is reinforced – a reward or reinforcement system.

Burrhus Skinner, born in Pennsylvania in 1904, was a leading behaviourist. He believed that people learn best by being rewarded by positive responses to an action or experience or demotivated by negative responses – as illustrated in his experiment with rats. The rats, in a special cage with a press-down bar on one side, accidentally find out that, if they press the bar, a food pellet is released. They then learn to do this again and again as and when they want food. When the rat presses the bar but no food is released, the rat learns to stop pressing the bar. Critics of behaviourism, however, point out that research in this area has been done only with animals and it, therefore, disregards any thought processes of which humans, but not animals, are capable.

Constructivism is based on the fact that, by observing and reflecting on new experiences, we can construct our own understanding of the world and, from that, each person generates his or her own rules, which are used to make sense of those experiences. Learning is, therefore, a search for meaning and meaning requires understanding of parts and wholes: parts must be understood in the context of wholes and wholes in the context of parts. It is for each individual to construct his or her own meaning rather than memorise the 'correct' answer or repeat someone else's answer.

The Swiss biologist and psychologist, Jean Piaget (1896–1980), was also very interested in the development of the child. His theory is based on the fact that children build up their own structures within the brain through their personal responses to a variety of physical experiences within their environment. He identified four hierarchical developmental stages.

1. Sensorimotor stage – the child builds up a set of concepts about reality and how it works, but does not realise that physical objects remain when out of sight.
2. Preoperational stage – the child cannot conceptualise abstractly and still needs physical and practical situations in order to make sense of new experiences.
3. Concrete operations – as the child accumulates experiences, he or she begins to explain their experiences; abstract problem solving is possible at this stage.
4. Formal operations – cognitive structures – the child is now able to reason and hypothesise, continually adjusting existing knowledge to accommodate new learning or experiences.

Lev Vygotsky (1896–1934), like Piaget, believed that learners moved through a hierarchical age-related scale of development. However, he insisted that learning was essentially a social activity in which learners are actively involved. His theory sees teachers as active participants in the promotion and development of learning, which he divides into two key areas.

- Specialised skill training, which involves the formation of a habit – for example, how to eat with a knife and fork, how to skip with a rope, etc.
- Activation of large areas of the brain's consciousness, involving thinking, reasoning, problem solving, investigation.

Constructivism would abolish a standardised curriculum in favour of a personalised one involving hands-on problem solving and open-ended questioning at all stages of development. In the *Five Year Strategy for Children and Learners*, Charles Clarke *promised to help meet individual needs . . . so there really are different and personalised opportunities available* (DfES, 2004, p7). Constructivists concentrate learning on making connections between facts and the promotion of assessment as part of the learning process rather than on standardised testing.

REFLECTIVE TASK

Think about your school or setting. Does it, in general, follow the principles of the behaviourist or social constructivist theory?

PRACTICAL TASK

Think of three differences between behaviourist and social constructivist theories. Complete the following table. The first one has been done for you.

SOCIAL CONSTRUCTIVIST	1. The child learns through problem solving
	2.
	3.
BEHAVIOURIST	1.
	2.
	3.

Indeed, it may occur in social constructivism that the teaching and learning roles may be reversed, as indicated in the following case study.

CASE STUDY 1

Three lads came to see me wanting to start a guitar club. They wanted space to do it and some support. They wanted to advertise it and run it themselves and a teacher to supervise it. It was a spur of the moment thing, but I suppose I intuitively recognised the opportunity it offered me. I volunteered to be the supervising teacher because I play the guitar myself. Badly, I have to say. As the supervising teacher I had nothing to do except keep an eye on things, watch and listen. I became a regular member. They were a million miles ahead of me in guitar technique. They recognised that pretty quickly, too, and helped me along from where I was, not from their pinnacle of expertise. Gently, but challengingly. They were excellent teachers. They taught me so much. I think I learned a bit, too, about organisation and teamwork and something about pedagogy as well.

(MacBeath and Myers, 1999)

In this case study the teacher/learner roles were reversed. The teacher felt unthreatened by the skills and knowledge of the pupils and, as a result of attending the sessions, not only increased his or her knowledge of playing the guitar, but also of *organisation, teamwork and pedagogy* (ibid.), too.

REFLECTIVE TASK

Why was it that the teacher in case study 1 felt unthreatened by the knowledge and skills of the children? Why do you think some teachers *may* feel threatened by this situation?

For effective learning, it is essential that learners take an active role in their learning, as the three boys did in case study 1. It is also important that learners know how they learn best.

PRACTICAL TASK

Complete the spider diagram: how do you learn best?

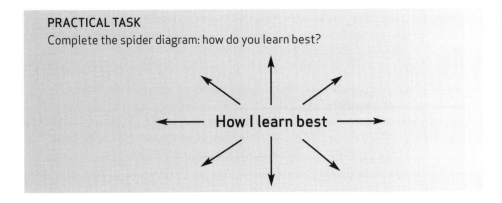

It is well documented that learners demonstrate increased self esteem, greater independence and ultimately higher achievement when they are involved in the development and understanding of their own learning experiences . . . When given greater opportunities for decision making and greater autonomy in their learning, they generally demonstrate greater motivation and perseverance.

(Pardoe, 2005, p8)

Lessons, therefore, should largely involve problem-solving activities. In this way, pupils can have the opportunity to investigate, research and discover information in their own way. Teachers should encourage discussion, debate, collaboration and co-operation. This further creates discussion and interaction between the pupils, who are then in control of their own learning. Discussion can be encouraged by effective questioning by the teacher. All questions should require thinking by the child; thinking extends learning.

PRACTICAL TASK

Turn these questions into 'thinking' questions. The first one is done for you.

Original question	Thinking question
What is the answer to 3764 – 1989?	Which of these is most likely to be the answer to 3764 – 1989? Why? 5753, 1775, 1795, 2775
Are drugs bad for you?	
Was Goldilocks naughty?	
Which ball bounces the highest?	
What is a complex sentence?	
Is it OK for a mother to steal food if her children are hungry?	

Learning styles and multiple intelligences

It is important to take account of the individual learning styles of the pupils. A learning style is the way in which each learner begins to concentrate on, process and retain new and difficult information. It is predetermined before the age of three or four and doesn't usually change throughout life.

Everyone has a learning style as individual as a fingerprint or signature, as a result of neural interconnection at the earliest stage of life. During this stage of development the basic architecture of the brain is established and learning styles are determined. Based on Sousa's analogy of the brain as a *jungle* (2000, p1), a person's preferred style is most likely to be the one they learned to use for survival as an infant, so their brain then gives it first priority for the rest of their lives. Very simply, most people understand the three modalities of visual, audio or kinaesthetic (VAK). However, many researchers, such as Ginnis (2002), see learning styles as divided into four basic areas: abstract, sequential, random and concrete, or, similarly, *activists, reflectors, theorists and pragmatists* (Honey and Mumford, 1992, p7). In general, most children and most adults fall somewhere between the areas and possess a combination of all four at different levels.

Concrete learners learn through doing, sensing and feeling; abstract learners learn through analysis and thought processes; active learners use a new experience in some way almost immediately; reflective learners learn through thought and reflection on experiences before acting.

Therefore, it is important for teachers to understand that some pupils like to research using books and record with writing; some like to investigate via the internet and represent their findings by a diagram or picture; some would like to represent their findings through modelling. Although it is important for pupils to have access to their own preferred style of learning, the teacher should ensure that a range of learning styles is available throughout the week, with pupils learning to work within a range of styles.

The essence of multiple intelligences is that there are many ways to learn and everyone is intelligent in their own way. With a multiple intelligence approach, intelligence is no longer reserved for those who can spell well, write well, compute difficult calculations or who have a high IQ, etc.

REFLECTIVE TASK

How you would describe 'intelligence'. Which children and adults you know are *intelligent*? What makes them intelligent?

CASE STUDY 2

It is a Monday morning in late autumn. The Year 3 class is timetabled for PE. It is cold out in the playground. The teacher has struggled into school with a sore throat and a headache. He is using hand signals to direct a surprisingly understanding group of shivering seven year olds. Mark is standing next to Thomas.

> *Mark has a spelling age of 14, reading level at 3a and a numeracy score of 4c. Pretty impressive tags. Thomas can read a handful of words, has just learned to count and has difficulty writing CVC words.*
>
> *The teacher wants Mark to collect a ball from the equipment store. In his voiceless state, he makes two gestures, one for 'Go over there', another for 'Pick up a ball'. Mark looks at his teacher blankly. In the best tradition of communication gone astray, the teacher makes the same signals again, only slower and with more detail. Mark still doesn't know what to do when the hands move for a third time. But Thomas, who has been watching all this time, turns to Mark and says, 'He wants you to go over there and get a ball.'*
>
> (Fleetman, 2006, p12)

REFLECTIVE TASK

In case study 2, who is more intelligent? Why?

Learning climate and motivation

It is vital to create a classroom where pupils are eager to learn, to discover what they don't know and where each day they can celebrate their successes; to create an atmosphere in which pupils feel safe to 'fail' and an atmosphere where 'I don't know' or 'I don't understand' is celebrated as a new opportunity to learn. Teachers need to build into pupils a sense of security – a safe haven. They need to hand over the learning to the pupils and support this by facilitating learning opportunities throughout each day – by scaffolding the learning less and less, as is suggested by Vygotsky's Zone of Proximal Development (1978). This can be seen as a continuum whereby the teacher supports the learner considerably at the outset. Eventually, the child needs the support of the teacher less and less.

An analogy for this would be learning to drive. At the start, the learner driver needs full support from a driving instructor. However, as the skill is practised, the learner driver needs the support of the instructor less and less until they can pass their driving test and are deemed qualified to drive. It involves developing a classroom in which the learner is responsible for his or her own learning – following a *constructivist model* (Clarke, 2004, p5). Teachers need to surrender control of the learning while still supporting and aiding the learning process. Teachers should be facilitators of learning rather than instructors, understanding the needs of the pupil implicitly. It is here that Abraham Maslow's Hierarchy of Needs (1943) is still very important today.

Maslow believed that the success of the learning environment was a vital factor in pupils' self-esteem and motivation to learn, and, in order for pupils to be at optimum learning capacity, all needs must be addressed.

- Physiological needs of the pupil – the needs of the body. This refers to having access to the toilet, to food and to drink, etc. As with adults, if the mind is concentrating on the fact that the body is hungry, thirsty or in need of a break or a visit to the toilet, learning is not going to take place; energies are focused on the physiological needs of the body.

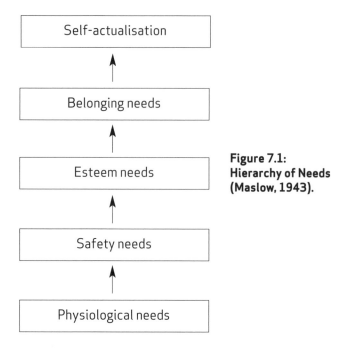

**Figure 7.1:
Hierarchy of Needs
(Maslow, 1943).**

- Safety needs – the need to feel secure, and that there is stability, familiarity and protection.
- Belonging needs – pupils need to feel that they belong, that they are accepted as part of the class, the year group and the school, and that they have friends. When they feel accepted, the brain will be released from the reptilian mode and be able to move to the limbic system, where the emotions, self-identity and values are uppermost. This is the area of the brain that controls long-term memory and attention.
- Esteem needs – all pupils need to feel that they are valued, respected and recognised and appreciated within the group; that every pupil has an important part to play in the team; and that all can be successful.

It is when all these areas are fulfilled that the pupil is ready to start to learn and to become more independent in their learning.

Therefore, the teacher needs to address the physical needs of the pupils – the need for regular breaks, for movement or brain gym, for water and food, for comfort of their workplace, and for the accommodation of different learning styles. Teachers need to accept pupil autonomy and initiative, allowing pupils to engage in discussion, debate and collaboration; and to ask open-ended questions and enquire why, how, where, what if, tell me more, explain further, etc.

CASE STUDY 3
A happy eight-year-old girl skipped to find her father, who was picking her up at the end of the school day. She chattered away to him about the fun she had had until she noticed that her dad was quiet. 'What is the matter?' she asked. 'I am very sorry,' her father said softly, 'I am afraid your rabbit has died during the day.' The little girl was devastated. She had had her rabbit as long as she could remember. Every day after school she fed her rabbit and played with him. Her evening was spent very

solemnly, not knowing what to do, how to feel, what to say. Very sad, she went to bed but found herself tossing and turning all night. As a result, in the morning, she was late getting up. She had to miss breakfast and could not find the homework she had done the night before. Her mum was trying to hurry her as she was going to be late for school. She quickly put on her shoes and coat and reluctantly left the house. She was rushing so much that soon she tripped and went crashing to the ground. Her knee was badly grazed and blood was trickling down her leg.

REFLECTIVE TASK

How do you think the little girl in case study 3 was feeling when she arrived at the school door? How would you feel in that situation? Is she ready to go into class and start her lessons? Why? What would you do?

Other factors affecting learning

According to Clarke (2005) the strategy that makes the most impact on learning is effective feedback. This is feedback that celebrates 'not knowing' as an opportunity for learning new things. In the case of young children, teachers could develop an area where children's new learning is acknowledged, such as a tree with leaves of new learning. Both oral and written feedback should contain a celebration of what is achieved and an area that could be improved in future. It is important, too, to allow the children the opportunity to assess their own and others' work. Children from a very young age are able to articulate what they like about their own or others' work and what they think could be done better the next time.

Some researchers insist that physical exercise plays a large part in making the brain ready to learn. Studies of the cerebellum (thought to be concerned with motor function) have now revealed that it is closely associated with spatial perception, language, attention, emotion, decision making and memory. The cerebellum forms only 10 per cent of the brain, but possesses over half of the brain's neurons. Movement and learning are, therefore, in a continual and complex interplay. Biologically, if a person is seated for 15 to 20 minutes, the blood flows to the feet and bottom. By standing up or moving about, the blood can be recirculated and, within just one minute, the flow of blood to the brain can increase by 15 per cent. It is, therefore, very important to have a classroom where the children are frequently able to move, to do a brain gym exercise, to be able to see, hear and do, and to learn through a variety of ways.

The essence of learning

With the recent development of initiatives such as assessment for learning, personalised learning, accelerated learning, emotional literacy and the social and emotional aspects of learning (SEAL) project, it is difficult to know which is effective in enhancing pupil learning, and which of the above initiatives or combinations of these or other initiatives to adopt. In essence, the above strategies are extremely similar. 'Assessment for learning' is about providing a safe, stimulating environment where pupils are confident learners and take control of their own targets for improvement.

'Personalised learning' is realising that one size does not fit all, and that equal is not fair. It is being able to allow pupils to feel that they are being given the opportunity to fulfil their view of their potential, identifying and responding to individual learning styles at a managerial, classroom and individual level. 'Accelerated learning' is based on the research over the last 15 years on how the brain works: we each have a preferred learning style – a way of learning that suits us best. If you know and use the techniques that match your preferred way of learning, you learn more naturally. Because it is more natural for you, it becomes easier; because it is easier, it is quicker; hence the name – *accelerated* learning. Both 'emotional literacy' and the 'social and emotional aspects of learning' (SEAL) project promote the fact that, unless the pupil is in an emotionally stable state, no learning will take place. The pupil needs to be able to articulate and discuss his or her emotions – fears, worries, sadness, as well as success, happiness and achievements.

Whatever approach you and your school take, it is important that pupils feel secure in the knowledge that, every time they approach a difficulty, it is a very special time that should be celebrated because new learning is about to take place.

It is vital that each classroom caters for personalised learning, tailoring education to individual needs, interests and aptitudes, to ensure that every pupil achieves and reaches the highest standards possible. It is shaping teaching around the way pupils learn. The learner must be given the navigation skills to cope with the journey. These include:

- the capacity to make *informed choices* and live with the consequences of those choices;
- the ability to *discriminate* between relevant and irrelevant information in a variety of contexts;
- the willingness to operate on a daily basis within a *moral code*;
- everyday *problem solving*;
- *active participation* in a number of communities.

And, throughout all the above:

- the ability to *feel positive* about themselves and others.

Each of the above strategies understands that each child is unique; that a single curriculum is not appropriate for all; and that pupils' needs should be taken into account in order to maximise the learning. At a conference of neuroscientists in Granada, Spain, the host (Ball, 2001), in his concluding statement, said:

> We need the science of pedagogy . . . If I can learn in a way that satisfies me, I will learn anything you want me to. But if I cannot learn in a way that is comfortable for me, then I will not learn anything, even if I want to learn it, let alone if you want me to learn it. The 'how' of my learning governs the 'what'. The pedagogy is more important than the curriculum.

CHAPTER SUMMARY

- Effective learning starts with knowledge of the child's needs.
- It is important to let the child have control of his or her own learning.
- Children learn best when they are relaxed and happy, and when they feel included and respected.

REFERENCES

Ball, E. (2001) 'Closing speech', 43rd International Meeting of the European Tissue Culture Society Cell Interactions and Cellular Complexity, Granada, Spain, 1–3 February.

Binet, A. and Simon, T. (1916/1973) *Human Intelligence*. Available online at www.indiana.edu/~intell/binet.shum (accessed 21 June 2008).

Clarke, S. (2004) *Enriching Feedback*. London: Hodder and Stoughton.

Clarke, S. (2005) *Formative Assessment in Action: Weaving the elements*. London: Hodder and Stoughton.

Department for Education and Skills (DfES) (2004) *Five Year Strategy for Children and Learners*. London: Crown.

Entwistle, N. (1996) *Styles of Learning and Teaching: An integrated outline of educational psychology for students, teachers and lecturers*. London: David Fulton.

Fleetham, M. (2006) *Multiple Intelligences in Practice*. Stafford: Network Continuum Education.

Ginnis, P. (2002) *The Teacher's Toolkit*. Glasgow: Bell & Bain.

Honey, P. and Mumford, A. (1992) *Manual of Learning Styles*. Maidenhead: Peter Honey.

Jensen, E. (2000) *Brain Based Learning*. San Diego, CA: The Brain Store.

MacBeath, J. and Myers, K. (1999) *Effective School Leaders*. London: Prentice Hall.

Maslow, A. (1943) A theory of human motivation. *The Psychological Review*, 50: 370–96.

Pardoe, D. (2005) *Towards Successful Learning*. Stafford: Network Educational Press.

Sousa, D. (2000) *How the Brain Learns*. Thousand Oaks, CA: Corwin Press.

Vygotsky, L.S. (1986) *Thought and Language* (ed. and trans. A. Kozulin). Cambridge, MA: MIT Press.

FURTHER READING

Alfrey, C. (ed.) (2003) *Understanding Children's Learning: A text for teaching assistants*. London: David Fulton.

Assessment Reform Group (2002) *Testing, Motivation and Learning*. Cambridge: University of Cambridge, Faculty of Education.

Black, P., Harrison, C., Lee, C., Marshall, B. and Wiliam, D. (2002) *Working Inside the Black Box*. London: Department of Education and Professional Studies, Kings College.

Bold, C. (2004) *Supporting Learning and Teaching*. London: David Fulton.

Carnell, E. and Lodge, C. (2002) *Supporting Effective Learning*. London: Paul Chapman.

De Freitas, S. and Yapp, C. (eds) (2005) *Personalizing Learning in the 21st Century*. Stafford: Network Educational Press.

Goleman, D. (1995) *Emotional Intelligence. Why it can matter more than IQ*. New York: Bantam Dell.

Kerry, T. and Wilding, M. (2004) *Effective Classroom Teacher: Developing the skills you need in today's classroom*. Edinburgh: Pearson Education.

Kyriacou, C. (1997) *Effective Teaching in Schools: Theory and practice*. Cheltenham: Stanley Thornes.

Kyriacou, C. (1998) *Essential Teaching Skills*. Cheltenham: Nelson Thornes.

Prashnig, B. (2006) *Learning Styles in Action*. Stafford: Network Continuum Education.

Smith, A. (1996) *Accelerated Learning in the Classroom*. Stafford: Network Educational Press.

Smith, A. (2004) *The Brain's Behind It*. Stafford: Network Educational Press.

Smith, A. and Call, N. (1999) *The Alps Approach: Accelerated learning in primary schools*. Stafford: Network Educational Press.

Smith, A., Lovatt, M. and Wise, D. (2003) *Accelerated Learning: A user's guide*. Stafford: Network Educational Press.

Watkinson, A. (2006) *Learning and Teaching: The essential guide for higher level teaching assistants*. London: David Fulton.

8 MANAGING CHANGE

Karen Castle

CHAPTER OBJECTIVES

By the end of this chapter you will:

- be able to identify how you will manage changes that take place in your work area;
- be able to identify the implications for managers when implementing change;
- have the opportunity to reflect on yourself as a change agent;
- begin to develop some understanding of why change is necessary.

LINKS TO **HLTA** STANDARDS

1. Demonstrate a commitment to collaborative and co-operative working with colleagues.
2. Improve their own knowledge and practice, including responding to advice and feedback.
3. Have sufficient understanding of specialist area(s) of expertise to support the development, learning and progress of children and young people.

Introduction

Change is an integral part of our daily lives and influences many of our decisions and activities, often to the extent that we rarely pause to reflect what effect change is really having on us and on those around us. According to Senge, *yesterday's solutions become today's problems* (1990, p57), suggesting that change is endemic and unavoidable. The capacity and ability to embrace change and to develop methods to enable us to accept and work with change has become an essential skill, and one that is necessary if we are to function successfully in modern society, and in the workplace.

This chapter will address some of the main issues surrounding change within an organisational context and, in so doing, will focus on change within an educational setting. It will discuss change from two perspectives: first, from the point of view of a manager, implementing change within the organisation; and, second, from the perspective of the individual employee, in identifying strategies to enable them to embrace and manage change from a personal standpoint.

Why do we need change?

Knowledge seems to widen and deepen at an ever-increasing rate, and we, as educational professionals, need to identify some way of managing how we cope with this information and innovation overload. People will form their own ways of dealing with this, which is why the management of change is a diverse and often fragmented area to understand.

In Chapter 2, you were asked to spend some time thinking about how things have changed in relation to the role of the teaching assistant (TA), or to discuss change with more experienced colleagues. Now you need not only to revisit these thoughts, but also to think about why the changes occurred.

Some social commentators will argue that we are moving from a modernist world – a world where structure, uniformity and hierarchy exist to provide a framework against which industry operates, and where family and work are separate entities, to a postmodern conception of the world and industry, where we experience fragmentation, alienation and uncertainty – a world in which work life and family life 'mesh' together and employers and organisations exercise more flexible, collegial and democratic ways of operation. Social theorists have suggested that postmodern society today is unpredictable and constantly changing, and that it can be volatile and chaotic. Morrison (1998) identified that many organisations employ managers whose roles increasingly involve managing this unpredictability, volatility and change. His name for this type of manager is 'impression manager'.

It would seem that change is inherent in a postmodern society, due to fragmentation and ever-changing bureaucratisation. However, despite this, many organisations are still clutching on to what is left of a modernistic framework and are, therefore, operating against the old and out-of-date 'factory' model. Hargreaves (1994) argues that most large educational institutions are typical of modernist organisations. Many operate a hierarchical structure; for example, with decision making being the sole preserve of the head teacher, and with a hierarchical approach to new innovations and ideas, using the National Curriculum as a framework against which to develop and deliver teaching could be perceived as a prescriptive format that has served to remove the autonomy of the teacher, in particular in terms of dictating the pedagogical element of teaching. It could be suggested, therefore, that schools need to change and adapt in order to become more flexible in the ways in which they meet the needs of pupils, students and staff, and this adaptation and flexibility could be viewed as precursors to becoming postmodern institutions. Furthermore, schools could become independently run units, dominated less by local authority bureaucracy and developing a more flexible approach to teaching and learning, maybe involving the local community. If the strategic and organisational aspect of the school is to change, the roles of the staff within the organisation will also need to undergo change.

For the purposes of this chapter, it is necessary to highlight, in particular, the role of the TA. It would seem that the role has changed dramatically over recent years, to encompass more responsibility and a greater range of tasks:

> *The teaching assistant now has a stronger role in the educational process as well as the more traditional roles of childcare, preparation, classroom organisation and pastoral care . . . teaching assistants need to be more flexible and innovative in order to meet the varied needs of their job. In successful schools, the role of the teaching assistant has developed to meet the needs*

of a more complex and demanding curriculum, larger teaching groups, a perceived increase in SEN pupils and increase in the level of formal assessment.

(Kay, 2005, p11)

Training and professional development for TAs has increased and become more focused in order to meet the demands of the new role. Higher Level Teaching Assistant (HLTA) status is awarded to those TAs who have successfully completed the HLTA training programme; similarly, foundation degrees provide a qualification structure for TAs to further their skills and career. It would, therefore, appear that significant changes have taken, and are taking place in the field of education, and it seems pertinent to suggest that those working within this environment need to identify and manage these changes successfully if the arena of education is to flourish.

CASE STUDY 1

Blackwater Secondary School is a large inner-city comprehensive school that has just been put into special measures following a less than satisfactory Ofsted inspection. One of the main areas of concern for the Ofsted inspectors was the apparent inflexibility of the organisation in responding to change. It was identified that the community within which the school is situated had changed considerably as there had been a high percentage of foreign families moving into the area. The increase in people who had English as a second language had impacted significantly on the community in general; however, the school had not identified with these changes, and was found to be lacking in several areas.

REFLECTIVE TASK

Give some consideration to case study 1 and reflect on the situation.

- What changes do you think the school could make in order to address the issue of foreign pupils?
- What impact would this have on staff at the school?
- What impact would this have on the pupils?
- What impact would this have on the community?

PRACTICAL TASK

Find out what the policy is in your school for pupils who have English as an additional language.

- Where is the policy kept?
- Is it easily accessible?

External influences

It has been argued that organisations need to change so that they are competitive in the marketplace. Most organisations operate against some degree of competition; retail outlets have historically needed to undercut or outsell their nearest competitor, or face a decline in profits. Service providers have traditionally experienced a less competitive approach, but this would appear to be changing. Educational institutions are often in competition with neighbouring training providers, whether independent, public or private sector, as the marketplace adapts to the changes in demand for the products or services. Businesses merge and, therefore, need to absorb change to enable the merger to be effective. Press publications routinely carry stories of business mergers or 'buy out' deals, often resulting in an insecure workforce and anxieties within the community. As a result in the falling pupil role of some schools, the education sector, from time to time, experiences school mergers. It, therefore, follows that staff within these schools will be feeling insecure as they apply for a limited number of posts within the newly merged school. Enabling these staff to positively embrace this type of change is extremely challenging. Parents and other stakeholders could be anxious, too, about mergers, particularly if they result in their children needing to travel further afield.

Political changes and initiatives from government at a national level will impact on organisations at a local level. External influences such as these are often unpredictable and therefore less able to be predetermined, which could result in managers and leaders being less able to demonstrate a proactive approach to change and, in some cases, appearing distant or remote from the change. It is very difficult for managers to plan for change that is, in some cases, unpredictable. However, Handy (2001) identified that managers need to keep a keen eye on the future and make changes appropriate to their judgement of what the future might hold. He went on to argue that the time at which they make a change is paramount to the change being effective. For example, if a manager left implementing change too late, they would be seen as a manager who led their workforce into decline; if they implemented the change too early, the perceived premature nature of the change may serve to convince the workforce that it is unnecessary.

CASE STUDY 2

The village of Cauldside has been investigating the possibility of having an 'out of school club'. The community want a safe and secure area for schoolchildren to access before and after their school day. At a recent village committee, it was decided to approach the three schools within the area, to ask if they would be interested in hosting such a club. Funding for this project will be met by the local government who have secured funding for five years. It is felt that this project will provide a degree of kudos for the school that is successful in its bid to host the club.

REFLECTIVE TASK

What could the schools in case study 2 do in order to ensure that they have a good chance of success in the bid to host the out of school club?

- What could be the schools' strengths?
- What could be the schools' weak areas?
- What changes would need to be considered by the heads of the schools?

Internal influences

Organisations need to be able to react to changes relating to their own strategies, often in response to a revision of goals or targets, or in response to making better use of resources. One of the most influential internal causes for innovation is the need for the organisation to change in order to improve standards. For example, a school may need to implement different strategies in order to respond to a recent OFSTED report. Performance management targets could impact on the way in which the staff appraisal process needs to change. Head teachers will need to implement changes to the way in which the school operates and, in so doing, may introduce new methods of working for the staff or new resources. Fullan (2007) reported that, in order to reform, schools need to do more that just put into place a new policy. Rather, they need to change the culture of the classroom and the organisation. Losing members of staff and gaining new members effects a change to the organisation, and this is happening every day in schools up and down the country. The existing staff will need to get used to the new dynamic that the staff changes will inevitably bring, and this means forging new relationships and interactions.

CASE STUDY 3
Primrose Dale is a large primary school that has recently been formed as a result of the merger of two small rural primary schools. The head teacher has recently held a consultative meeting with staff to discuss how they view the future of the school. One of the main issues discussed was the changing role of the TAs. It would seem that, prior to the merger, the TAs at both of the smaller schools were responsible for such duties as assisting the teacher with tasks such as preparing art and craft resources, helping with photocopying, supporting some of the children in lessons with reading and writing, helping to prepare lessons and looking after children who were ill. The head teacher now wanted the TAs to change their role, and take part in professional development activities that would enable them to have greater responsibility and more accountability.

PRACTICAL TASK
Discuss with your head teacher, or deputy head, the organisational policy for implementing change. Find out how internal change is disseminated to staff.

Change in an educational context

It would seem, therefore, pertinent to argue that organisations need to change in response to a variety of influences. Educational settings, being organisations themselves, also need to change. During the 1980s and 1990s, changes to educational policy in terms of the devolution of budget control and marketisation forced the management of schools to become more focused on a business model. In conflict with this, Wilby (1997) argued that education should not initiate business practices, as business is seen as less than moral. It is often undemocratic and obsessed with image as opposed to substance, being driven by profit. There are many and varied arguments comparing the business and educational models, and this chapter will not address these is any depth; however, it is apt to appreciate that these arguments exist and are often the catalyst for educational change today.

It is probably fair to say that education has changed considerably over the past few years, both from a curriculum point of view and from a strategic perspective. Watkinson (2003) has identified that the practices of the past and people's attitudes to work will need to change in order to adapt to future developments. She has found that the new role of the TA will require them to work much more closely with teaching staff.

From 1992 to 2000 there was a 112 per cent increase in the volume of education support staff in primary schools in England, the great majority being classroom assistants (DfES, 2000). Later, in 2004, there were 133,440 full-time equivalent TAs working in mainstream and special schools (DfES, 2005).

The government has proposed that the increasing demands on classroom teachers will be alleviated by the TA, in terms of HLTAs covering classes in order that teachers can be released to perform other tasks (DfES, 2003). It further suggests that the classroom is *no longer the sole preserve of the teacher* (DfES, 2003, p6).

CASE STUDY 4
Dunromin Secondary School has just received training school status, and as a result will be the central school for continuing professional development (CPD) and training for education professionals within the area. It will also be able to offer the graduate teaching programme. The change in status of the school has led to the head teacher making changes to the way in which the school approaches CPD. This, in turn, has led to several HLTAs taking lessons and performing many of the tasks that were once the domain of the teacher. This has been received well by the majority of staff, but there are a few staff who have reacted quite negatively towards the change to the role of the TAs.

Change from the point of view of the individual

People are often called upon to adapt to new ways of working, learn new tasks and embrace new technology. Once the change is implemented they must learn to cope with the impact the change has on them and on their role. It is important to realise that people will need time to adapt to new systems and processes. People generally develop their performance gradually and over different periods of time depending on the individual. Carnall (2003) has argued that significant organisational changes can create a decline in self-esteem. If we understand that workers in any organisation become more confident in their role as they build up a wealth of understanding and knowledge developed from their experience and skills, we can see that their confidence could easily become disrupted if they need to learn new skills or operate under unfamiliar regimes. I would argue strongly that people need support and guidance though the change, and that they need to feel safe through the process of change, not just at the implementation stage, but consistently throughout. Furthermore, people need to know how they have managed the change; they need to receive objective feedback on their actions.

Peer support can offer workers the opportunity to discuss problems and anxieties in a non-threatening environment, maybe by introducing humour in order to lighten the situation and to help in discovering coping mechanisms. Many workers will be terrified of making a mistake or showing themselves up in front of colleagues, particularly when they have previously been able to carry out tasks almost as second nature.

Coping with change requires the individual to identify coping strategies. Prior to this, the individual needs to be able to understand themselves and, in so doing, to reflect on such issues as: How will I be affected by this change? Am I going to be able to accept the change? What is the worst thing that can happen to me? What will be of most benefit to me?

If the change involves a different job role, the individual needs to identify what skills and abilities are needed for the new role and if they are able to develop their own skills. They may need help in doing this, but they may not always acknowledge their need for help.

Where the change involves working with different people, the individual needs to reflect on their own communication and interaction skills – do these need to be developed? Has this situation happened before and, if so, how did the individual react in that situation? Very often we don't fully appreciate the skills that we have used in previous situations and that are transferable to current events.

CASE STUDY 5

Reuben has been a TA for five years. He has just begun to study for a foundation degree in supporting teaching and learning and has been supported in his CPD by the head teacher. Reuben has identified that he would like to take part in any of the school's developmental activities and has been pro-active in identifying such opportunities. The head teacher therefore asked Reuben if he would take a leading role in introducing the interactive whiteboard to the classroom. The head wants to put whiteboards in every classroom and has realised the need for staff to be trained in the use of the board. The head has informed Reuben that he will attend a training course and then return to the school to train the other members of staff in the use of the board.

Reuben, however, is very anxious about training the other staff, as he feels somewhat intimidated by some of the other teachers. He is happy with the fact that he will learn about the new innovation, but is less confident with his skills as a trainer.

REFLECTIVE TASK

- Reflecting on case study 5, what would you do if you were in Reuben's position, and why would you act in such a way?
- How differently could the head teacher have approached this?
- Think about how you respond to change in different situations. Do you, for example, react differently to change at work than you would to a change in your social arrangements?
- How would you respond to a change to your working hours – a situation that may impact on your home life and family? Why would you react in this way?

PRACTICAL TASK

Select a group of colleagues and social contacts and find out from them how they personally respond to change. Design a small questionnaire and ask each of them to complete it. Once you have received their responses, give some thought to what they have said.

Resistance to change

There appears to be a deep-seated belief that change is difficult; that it is something to be feared, or to feel threatened by. Some authors argue that people are conditioned to be resistant to change. But why might this be the case? Carnall (2003) argues that resistance to change is derived from the mismanagement of the introduction of change. If people understand what is expected of them, what the outcomes of the change are likely to be and the impact on them as individuals, it seems that resistance to change may be lessened. An organisation in which shared goals are not experienced could be at a disadvantage in terms of achieving a workforce that embraces change. For example, the senior management goals might be to increase the number of pupils achieving a pass at a certain level, whereas the goal of a certain class teacher may be focused on improving literacy. Some people may be resistant to change as they have had previous bad experiences of having to deal with it, or maybe they resist change as it will impact on their family. For example, if a manager wants to implement an extended day, the hours that workers will need to work will change. This could impact on family and social life.

In a recent survey carried out by the author into the way in which CPD has been introduced to school staff, the following responses were among the data received:

- 'Why do I need to start doing this? It won't make a difference to my salary, won't guarantee job security.'
- 'I've been teaching this way for 12 years. I have not had a poor appraisal, so why should I change now?'
- 'If it isn't one thing it's another. Why can't we just leave things alone, and allow ourselves to catch up to where we need to be? It seems to me that you are introducing change for change's sake, particularly when we are so busy just trying to maintain the status quo.'

It seems that, faced with change, people find real value and pertinence in their present situation. Sayings such as: 'If it isn't broken, why fix it?' and 'Don't change a winning team' often resonate from staff rooms.

CASE STUDY 6

Bella Cairn is 55 and has been a TA for 30 years. She is well liked by the children and staff and is respected within the village community in which the school is situated. Bella decided not to take part in any professional development as she felt that, as she had been working in school for so long, she didn't really need to learn anything more. She had never had a bad report from the head and had constantly been told that she does a good job. Bella had always found it difficult to understand why other TAs would want to take part in any training courses or programmes, and had often told them that they were wasting their time and what they were learning would change anyway.

REFLECTIVE TASK

Think about case study 6 and reflect on why Bella might be feeling this way.

- Why would she pass her negative feelings on to other TAs who could quite easily be influenced by her?
- How could the other TAs respond to her?

Now imagine that you are a teaching assistant working with Bella and you have just begun to study for a foundation degree. How might you feel as a result of what Bella is saying and how would you handle this situation?

Change from the point of view of a manager

The ways in which the school is managed, in terms of the style of leadership and management demonstrated by the head teacher and deputies, affect and impact on the way in which change is received by the workforce within the school. People need to feel that change in necessary, and that it isn't implemented for the sake of it. Workers often feel that change is made by managers purely to justify their own positions within the hierarchy of the organisation, or as a 'knee jerk' reaction to internal or external influences. Managers and leaders responsible for change need to identify clear and effective communication systems within the organisation. If there are poor communication channels, or if managers are 'out of reach' of the workforce, anxieties and concerns that the workforce have will not be aired and are, therefore, likely to become significant issues as time progresses. Workers need to feel that they are important to the overall effectiveness and success of the organisation. Only when workers feel safe and unthreatened are they likely to embrace change in a manner that is appropriate to the organisation as a whole. Similarly, the workforce needs to feel supported through the change process. As mentioned earlier, workers need time to adjust to the change, and managers will benefit from giving time to their staff, and supporting them through the change.

Take some time to consider the scenario in case study 7, which is taken from a true situation.

CASE STUDY 7
A special needs unit within a large secondary school had been earmarked for closure. The unit was managed by a Special Educational Needs Co-ordinator (SENCO), supported by teachers and teaching assistants. The staff had been told that the unit was probably going to have to restructure and that this would impact on their roles in the future. They were informed that it was unlikely that they would be made redundant, as they would be needed to support the children with special needs in the respective classrooms. The SENCO had voiced the concerns of the staff on several occasions, the unit staff were concerned that their jobs were no longer secure and several of the teachers from other areas were concerned that the children with special needs would have a detrimental impact on their classes. One Monday morning, the unit staff opened their e-mails to learn that the unit would close at the end of that term (in approximately four weeks' time). The head teacher had informed them by e-mail of this and had asked them, if they had any questions or queries, to make an appointment with him the following day.

This situation led to the SENCO resigning and several of the other staff feeling aggrieved and undervalued.

PRACTICAL TASK

Talk to the head teacher or deputy head teacher at your school and ask them to discuss with you their view of managing change. How would they implement change to the school workforce? What do they think are the most important things to remember?

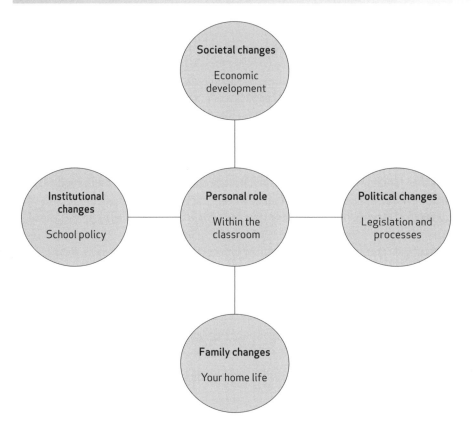

Figure 8.1: A metaphor for change (adapted from Tyrer et al., 2004)

REFLECTIVE TASK

Have a look at Figure 8.1 and place yourself in the middle circle. How are you affected by the three driving forces for change?

PRACTICAL TASK

Think about a recent change that you were involved with:

- in your school;
- in your classroom;
- with a pupil.

Now answer the following.

- Who or what generated the change?
- How was the change implemented?
- Who supported the change? And how?

- Who resisted the change? And how?
- What was your role in the change?
- How did the situation conclude?
- What have you learned from this about change and how to handle it?

CHAPTER SUMMARY

- The role of the TA has changed significantly over the past few years.
- There are many different catalysts for change and these impact on the individual and the organisation in different and diverse ways.
- Managing change can be approached from different angles: for example, from the point of view of the manager or change agent implementing the change, and from the point of view of the individual in managing the way that change impacts on them and their role.
- Some people will support and react positively to change, while others will resist or reject change.
- If change is to be effective, it must influence and be influenced by the values of the staff and the organisation.
- Change cannot be hurried or rushed through. It needs to take time, to give people the opportunity to digest the change and seek support and guidance as necessary.
- Change is too important to leave to the experts.

REFERENCES

Carnall, C. (2003) *Managing Change in Organisations* (4th edn). London: Prentice Hall.

Department for Education and Skills (DfES) (2000) *Time for Standards: Reforming the school workforce*. London: DfES.

Department for Education and Skills (DfES) (2003) *Developing the Role of School Support Staff*. London: DfES.

Department for Education and Skills (DfES) (2005) *Statistics of Education, Schools in England*. London: DfES.

Fullan, M. (2007) *The New Meaning of Educational Change* (4th edn). London: Routledge.

Handy, C. (2001) *The Empty Raincoat*. London: Random House.

Hargreaves, A. (1994) *Changing Teachers, Changing Times*. London: Teachers College Press.

Kay, J. (2005) *Teaching Assistant's Handbook (Primary Edition)*. London: Continuum.

Morrison, K. (1998) *Managing Theories for Educational Change*. London: Paul Chapman.

Senge, P. (1990) *The Fifth Discipline*. New York: Random House.

Tyrer, L., Gunn, S., Lee, C., Parker, M., Pitman, M. and Townsend, M. (2004) *A Toolkit for the Effective Teaching Assistant*. London: Paul Chapman.

Watkinson, A. (2003) *The Essential Guide for Competent Teaching Assistants: Meeting the national occupational standards at level 2*. London: David Fulton.

Wilby, P. (1997) Stopping the clocks on inequality will not stem it. *Times Education Supplement*, 28 November.

FURTHER READING

Handy, C. (1993) *Understanding Organisations*. London: Penguin.

Whitaker, P. (1999) *Managing Schools*, Oxford: Butterworth.

9 TEACHING AND SUPPORTING READING/SYNTHETIC PHONICS

Elizabeth Kirtlan and Jean Bedford

CHAPTER OBJECTIVES

By the end of this chapter you will:

- understand the current practice and theories linked to the development of reading in children;

- be aware of synthetic phonics programmes;

- identify and reflect on strategies to support pupils who are exhibiting reading difficulties.

LINKS TO **HLTA** STANDARDS

1. Have high expectations of children and young people with a commitment to helping them fulfil their potential.

2. Improve their own knowledge and practice, including responding to advice and feedback.

3. Understand the key factors that affect children's and young people's learning and progress.

4. Know how to contribute to effective personalised provision by taking practical account of diversity.

5. Have sufficient understanding of their area(s) of expertise to support the development, learning and progress of children and young people.

6 Understand the objectives, content and intended outcomes for the learning activities in which they are involved.

7. Devise clearly structured activities that interest and motivate learners and advance their learning.

8. Contribute to the selection and preparation of resources suitable for children's and young people's interests and abilities.

Introduction

This chapter examines current practice and theories linked to the development of reading in children. It will discuss the rationale and reintroduction of synthetic phonics programmes and will enable you to identify and select effective support strategies for those pupils experiencing reading difficulties.

The development of reading

Learning to read is a complex matter, but it is widely agreed that interesting children in literacy through a variety of fun activities from the Early Years is significant:

> *For the youngest children, well before the age of five, sharing and enjoying favourite books regularly with trusted adults, be they parents, carers, practitioners or teachers, is at the heart of this activity. Parents and carers should be strongly encouraged in these pursuits and reassured that, in so doing, they are contributing massively to children's literacy and to their education in general.*
>
> (DfES, 2006, p4)

Children learn and develop as individuals and this applies equally to their learning to read. In the early phases they will act out reading behaviour by holding the book, looking at the words and pictures and turning pages. They will later begin to understand that the words carry meaning and point to familiar words. As they progress further they will:

- retell and read familiar texts;
- attempt unfamiliar texts by reading word for word;
- start sounding out and using picture cues to help them.

They will then begin to employ various strategies to enable them to read different types of texts before finally becoming independent readers, by which time strategies are applied automatically.

According to Ann Browne, the foundation for reading is traditionally established between the ages of four and eight, *but the process begins before this and continues after it* (2002, p26). She goes on to say:

> *Learning to read does not necessarily begin at 4, neither does it end at 8. All children need supported experiences with books and practice at reading a variety of texts before they are fluent.*
>
> (ibid., p27)

This is also iterated in *Early Years Foundation Stage* by the DCSF, who say that at 22–36 months children will be *looking at picture books and listening to stories, important steps in literacy* (DCSF, 2007).

Before they come to school, children will have been exposed to a great deal of print in many contexts, from reading stories in their homes, to seeing signs on shops and being able to spot their favourite brand of breakfast cereal. It is, therefore, important to start with what the child already knows. *Children need to understand that reading is enjoyable and informative and relevant to their present lives* (ibid., p38). This is echoed by Kathy Hall, who writes, *learners have to understand and believe that reading is important for them in the here and now of their lives* (Hall, 2003, p194).

So how can we as practitioners help support and develop the reading skills of the children we are working with? Consider the following two statements; the first taken from the Bullock Report of 1975 and the second again from Ann Browne:

> *there is no one method, medium, approach, device or philosophy that holds the key to the process of learning to read.*
>
> (DES, 1975, p77)

> *there is still no single description of the reading process or one agreed way of helping children to become readers.*
>
> (Browne, 1998, p1)

REFLECTIVE TASK

What do you think about these statements? What teaching methods and strategies are you aware of or do you employ in your setting to help children to learn to read? How do you ensure that you start with what the child already knows?

In the Foundation Stage, effective teaching requires practitioners to demonstrate *the use of language for reading and writing . . . through telling stories and sharing books in a clear and lively way that motivates children* (DfEE, 2000, p46). *Children will begin to learn that reading in English is from left to right and top to bottom and begin to recognise favourite phrases* (ibid., p47). By the end of the Foundation Stage, children are expected to be able to *read a range of familiar and common words and simple sentences independently* (DCSF, 2007). The 'prime approach' used to achieve this is phonics, which will be discussed later in this chapter.

By the end of Year 2, the DCSF believe, *the development of children's phonic knowledge, skills and understanding is time limited and the majority of children will usually achieve the learning objectives . . . by the end of Key Stage 1* (DCSF, 2008). The emphasis then switches from word recognition to language comprehension and, by the end of Key Stage 2, the objective is for children to read extensively and discuss their reading with others.

As children progress through Key Stages 3 and 4, the new Secondary Framework for English places the emphasis on 'reading for meaning', using a range of strategies and the ability to *analyse, compare and respond to layers of meaning, subtlety and allusion in texts and contrast texts* (DCSF, 2008, p13).

The question that still remains is, how do we teach reading? You may be surprised to learn that the debate between 'whole word' teaching methods and phonics is not new. In America in the late 1800s, a phonic series of books known as McGuffy Readers was very popular (Snowling and Hulme, 2007). These books reviewed previously taught letter sounds and then introduced new ones. An alternative method of teaching reading and spelling instructs the child *to think little h is the picture of the chair Bess sits in when she is very tired. As she sits down she breathes very hard, h, h, h* (ibid., p502). Those of you familiar with Jolly Phonics may recall the action for 'h' – 'Hold hand in front of mouth panting as if you are out of breath and say *h, h, h*' (Lloyd and Wernham, 2005).

These methods were not embraced by all and most notably not by the American educational reformer Horace Mann, who, in 1842, wrote *When we wish to give a child the idea of a new animal we do not present successively the different parts of it – an eye, an ear, . . . but we present the whole animal as one object* (Snowling and Hulme, 2007, p503). Frank Smith also argued that *systematic phonics is destined to fail as a method of reading instruction, and will make learning to read more difficult for many children* (1999, p151).

So the debate continued with the whole word approach dominating the scene in the early to mid twentieth century, with the *emphasis on authentic children's literature and the minimising of phonics or phonics-influenced texts* (Snowling and Hulme 2007, p507), as the latter were considered relatively boring.

PRACTICAL TASK

Take a look at the range of books and other materials used in your setting to teach reading. Are you able to identify a phonic or whole word approach? What about the stories, illustrations and styles? Do they match the levels of interest for the children you work with? Make a short list using the table below (the first one has been completed for you as an example).

Title	Scheme/ Author	Whole word/ Phonic	Age band (if given or best guess)	Readability
Cat in a bag	Oxford Reading Tree	Phonic and high-frequency words	4–5	Lots of colourful pictures to add interest for this age group

We must also think carefully about ourselves as role models when it comes to developing an interest in reading for the children in our schools. Do they see us reading for purpose and enjoyment? Or are we too focused on the mechanics of reading? Consider this statement from Kathy Hall:

the way they are taught reading conveys to them powerful messages about what reading is and what it is good for.

(2003, p194)

She also adds this cautionary note:

Teaching reading is not a simple task and any teacher who thinks that any one model, scheme or programme will simplify this task or will suit all learners is grossly naïve.

(ibid., p191)

Introduction to synthetic phonics programmes

What is synthetic phonics?

Synthetic phonics is one approach to teaching phonics to children. It is seen to be particularly appropriate for children beginning schooling, where they are yet unable to read and nearly all written words are unfamiliar to them. The term 'synthetic' in synthetic phonics means to 'synthesise' (i.e. put together or build up) pronunciations for unfamiliar written words by translating letters into sounds and blending the sounds together ('blending' = 'synthesising').

Synthetic phonics is used in Germany and Austria and is generally taught before children are introduced to books or reading. It is said that this approach works well in Germany, where there is a regular spelling system; however, the irregular spelling system we have in the English language is thought to not work as effectively. For example, 'yacht' is an irregular word and, if a child tries to sound this out, there might be a 'ch' sound in it, as in 'cheese' (Johnston and Watson, 2007). However, Adams (1990) stated that 80–90 per cent of words in English do have regular spellings, so this method could be put into practice.

Synthetic phonics teaches children the letter sounds quite rapidly, and a number of letter sounds are learnt very quickly after starting school. When the first few letter sounds have been taught, children are shown how to blend them together to pronounce unfamiliar words (Feitelson, cited in Johnston and Watson, 2007). In a UK version of synthetic phonics, i.e. *Hickey Multi-Sensory Language Course* (Augur and Briggs, 1992), the first block of letter sounds is 's', 'a', 't', 'i', 'p' and 'n', which make up more three-letter words than any other six letters. An example of this is that, when the children have learnt these letter sounds, they are able to blend these letters into words such as 'at', 'pat', 'tap', 'sat', pin' 'tin' and so on.

In 1998, Johnston and Watson undertook a study in Clackmannanshire to examine the effects of three types of phonics programmes on the reading and spelling of children in their first year of school (Primary 1 in Scotland, equivalent to Reception in England). The programmes lasted for 16 weeks, for 20 minutes a day. At the end of the study, the findings showed that those children who were taught the synthetic phonics programme were seven months ahead for their age in word reading and spelling (Johnston and Watson, 2005).

These are the thoughts of a teacher who first used the synthetic phonics programme in Clackmannanshire:

From these sessions my first impression was that of speed. The pace of the lessons was very slick and well structured. Letters and Sounds were introduced with up to four new sounds a week, which was much quicker than any approach I had previously experienced . . . Children were active and interacting in the lessons: finding letters, blending words and forming letters. The children's enthusiasm and sense of achievement was electric and impressed me greatly.

(Macnair, cited in Lewis and Ellis, 2006, p187)

Following the pilot of synthetic phonics in Clackmannanshire and the Rose Review (2006), which will be discussed below, a new programme was introduced in English schools.

Rose Review

Research into the best way to teach reading was undertaken by Jim Rose on behalf on the Department for Education and Skills (DfES, 2006). His final report was published in 2006, giving guidance on future policy on the teaching of reading in England. This study arose from many recommendations around the National Literacy Strategy (NLS) and *what methods schools used to teach reading* (House of Commons Education and Skills Committee, 2004). The Clackmannanshire study, as discussed previously, was also highlighted in one of the recommendations made by the House of Commons Education and Skills Committee, as one of the reasons why a comparative study into the teaching of synthetic phonics with the NLS should be completed.

As a result of the recommendations, the DfES asked Jim Rose and a panel of advisers to:

examine current evidence about practices for teaching children to read to ensure the Strategy can continue to provide the most effective support assuring children's progression in reading.

(DfES, 2005)

Below are highlighted the five aspects the Rose Review committee examined, together with their findings of these, which were published in the final report (adapted from Lewis and Ellis, 2006).

1. What best practice should be expected in the teaching of the early reading and synthetic phonics.
   - Priority and clear guidance should be given to developing children's speaking and listening skills.
   - High-quality, systematic phonic work as defined by the review should be taught discretely as the prime approach in learning to decode (to read) and encode (to write/spell) print.
   - Phonic work should be set within a broad and rich language curriculum.
   - The Primary National Strategy should continue to exemplify the kind of teaching all children should experience (quality-first teaching).

2. How this relates to the development of the Early Years Foundation Stage and the development and renewal of the National Literacy Strategy *Framework for Teaching*.
   - For most children, high-quality, systematic phonic work should start by the age of five. This should be multi-sensory.
   - The Searchlight model of reading should be reconstructed.

- The Early Years Foundation Stage and the renewed literacy framework must be compatible with each other and give guidance on the continuity and progression in phonic work.

3. What range of provision best supports children with significant literacy difficulties and enables them to catch up with their peers, and the relationship of such targeted intervention programmes with synthetic phonic teaching.
   - High-quality phonic work should be a priority within normal classroom teaching.
   - Additional support should be compatible within mainstream practice.
   - Interventions should be matched to the different types of special educational needs.

4. How leadership and management in schools can support the teaching of reading, as well as practitioners' subject knowledge.
   - Leaders should make sure that phonic work is given appropriate priority in the teaching of beginner readers.
   - At least one member of staff should be able to lead on literacy, especially phonic work.
   - Leaders should monitor the quality and consistency of phonic work and give staff feedback.

5. The value for money or cost-effectiveness of the range of approaches the review considers.
   - Develop a series of additional training of teachers with in-service training and with LA.
   - Increase professional development opportunities to also increase teacher, trainee and TA knowledge about early reading, particularly phonics.

REFLECTIVE TASK

Using the list above containing the recommendations, how have these been implemented in your school setting? What impact have they made?

Letters and Sounds

In 2007, the DfES published a new programme to aid the teaching of synthetic phonics, named *Letters and Sounds*: *Principles and practice of high quality phonics*, which replaced *Playing with Sounds* and *Progression in Phonics*. This is one of many high-quality phonics teaching programmes that meet the core criteria set out by the DfES (2006). *Letters and Sounds* is based on the 'simple view of reading' outlined in the Rose Review (DfES, 2006). This identifies two dimensions of reading – 'word recognition' and 'language comprehension'.

The 'simple view' shows that, to become proficient readers and writers, children must develop both word recognition and language comprehension. This programme focuses on securing word recognition skills as these are essential for children to decode (read) and encode (spell) words accurately. This process then concentrates on comprehending and composing text (DfES, 2007).

The *Letters and Sounds* programme enables children to see the relationship between reading and spelling, with the teaching of one reinforcing the understanding of the other. It is structured into

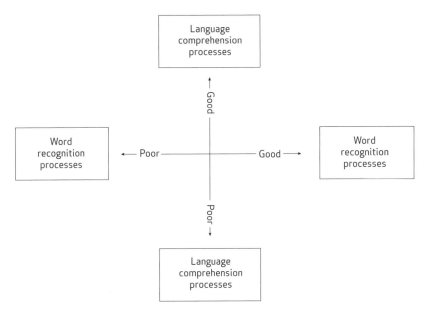

Figure 9.1: Simple view of reading model

six phases: *Letters and Sounds: Notes of guidance* makes it clear that the boundaries between each phase are not fixed. Detailed below is a brief summary of each phase.

Phase 1

Phase 1 is not part of the phonic teaching programme but prepares children for phonic work. This phase is to be carried out in the Early Years Foundation Stage where speaking and listening skills are developed. Activities are included to develop oral blending and segmenting of the sounds of spoken words.

Phase 2

Phonic teaching starts to take place in this phase, where 19 letters of the alphabet are taught. Pupils learn the visual appearance, the sounds and the formation of these letters. The main focus in this stage is that children understand that blending and segmenting are reversible processes.

Pupils use sounding and blending for reading, converting the letters into sounds, for example the word 'sat'. The child knows the letter sounds 's', 'a' and 't', so by saying them from left to right and then blending them together, the child identifies the word as 'sat'.

Children will be able to segment for spelling, where the child hears the word and then breaks it down into its component sounds. For example, when learning to read the word 'tap', the child will take each sound in turn and take the relevant letter each time to form the word: 't', 'a' and 'p'. The child will blend the letter sounds together to check they have the correct spelling and word.

By doing these processes, children will soon by able to read and spell simple Vowel Consonant (VC) and Consonant Vowel Consonant (CVC) words.

Phase 3

This phase complete the letters of the alphabet. It also introduces sounds represented by more than one letter, for example 'oa', 'ow' and 'ar'. Children also continue to practise CVC blending and segmenting and also apply this knowledge to reading and spelling two-syllable words and captions.

Phase 4

In this phase, children consolidate their knowledge of graphemes in reading and spelling words containing adjacent consonants; examples of these are 'jump', 'went' and 'frog'.

Phase 5

The purpose of this phase is to broaden the children's knowledge of graphemes and phonemes for use in reading and spelling. They learn new graphemes and alternative pronunciations for these. An example of this is 'ow' – cow, blow.

Phase 6

By the time children reach this phase, they should be able to read hundreds of words. During this phase, children become fluent readers and increasingly accurate spellers. It is also focused on looking more at word-specific spellings and making choices between spelling alternatives.

Having detailed briefly the different phases of *Letters and Sounds*, below is the sequence of teaching for each discrete phonics session of Phase 3.

Introduction   • Objectives and criteria for success.
Revisit and review   • Practise previously learned letters or graphemes.
Teach   • Teach new graphemes.   • Teach one or two tricky words.
Practise   • Practise blending and reading words with a new Grapheme–Phoneme Correspondence (GPC).   • Practise segmenting and spelling words with a new GPC.
Apply   • Read or write a caption or sentence using one or more tricky words and words containing the graphemes.
Assess learning against criteria

REFLECTIVE TASK

At school, observe a phonics session, noting the pace of the session and progression made by the children during it. Reflect on the phonics approaches taught within your school setting.

The next section of the chapter will be discussing in detail aspect 3 of the Rose Review: intervention programmes for children displaying reading difficulties.

Children experiencing reading difficulties

For many years, experts have studied to find reasons why children experience reading difficulties. For many teachers, children's failure to make good progress in reading is a main area of concern. Browne (2002, p191) comments on how the difficulties manifest themselves in a number of ways and points out that some children may have several types of difficulty. She explains this further by stating that, until the reading difficulty and its cause have been analysed, it is hard to provide the appropriate help and support. Browne found five possible types of reading difficulty (ibid., p192); these are:

1. being unable to read;
2. not wanting to read;
3. not understanding what is read;
4. thinking one can't read;
5. not reading the texts provided.

But questions may be asked as to what causes these types of reading difficulties. Browne identifies three sets of possible factors that often contribute to failure in learning to read (ibid., p192). The following demonstrates these factors.

Physical factors
- Visual impairment.
- Hearing problems.
- Language delay or disorder.
- Ill health resulting in prolonged or frequent absence from school.
- Environmental factors.
- High adult expectations and pressure.
- Absence of books at home.
- Unfavourable home circumstances.

School factors
- Irrelevant materials.
- Teacher expectations too high.
- Teacher expectations too low.
- Purpose for reading not clear to the children.
- Poorly organised reading programme.
- Teachers responding negatively to children who are slow to start reading.

Personal characteristics
- Anxiety.
- Lack of motivation.
- Short attention span.
- Poor self-image.
- Not understanding what reading is for.
- General learning difficulties.

REFLECTIVE TASK

Think of a child in your setting who you feel is experiencing reading difficulties. Using the list above, can you identify any possible factors that could contribute to this?

Myers and Burnett (2004) agree with Browne (2002) in that, when children display difficulties in reading, this limits their access to literature and the wider curriculum. Like Browne, they also identify some of the problems children have with reading; these include lack of:

- interest;
- confidence;
- phonic skills;
- reading for meaning;
- the ability to recall letters and high-frequency words.

It is essential that children escape this cycle of failure and experience the pleasures of reading and a sense of achievement. There are many ways in which reading difficulties can be overcome, but these involve careful planning of tasks, selection of texts and the provision of support. Children can then see that reading is a meaningful activity (Myers and Burnett, 2004, p221). Many of the contributing factors outlined above can be corrected; for example, physical factors can often be corrected or helped by referring the child for a sight or hearing test. Other physical problems need to be addressed individually, but this does not mean that the child cannot or will not read. Environmental difficulties may be solved by the school working closely with the parents and carers in order to find ways to help the child to read and develop interests in reading.

REFLECTIVE TASK

Think of a child who is making good progress in reading. Why do you think that is? Compare these factors with a child who is experiencing reading difficulties. What are the differences? What steps could you put in place to help overcome these?

Myers and Burnett (2004, p222) offered suggestions for supporting children with reading difficulties.

Supporting children who lack interest, enthusiasm and confidence in reading

This can be encouraged through:

- frequent reading aloud by the teacher of a wide range of texts;
- provision of carefully selected texts that relate to children's interests;
- opportunities to read to younger children;
- opportunities to share books with friends and listen to tapes.

Supporting children in reading for meaning

This can be encouraged through:

- opportunities to share and discuss texts of interest with friends;
- cloze procedure and activities to develop responses;
- focused activities of interest, such as a headline for a newspaper report, an e-mail or a text message to a friend.

Supporting children in recalling letters and recognising high-frequency words

Developing visual discrimination can be encouraged through:

- matching games, snap or bingo;
- discussing shapes of letters and words;
- highlighting a letter or high-frequency word in a text;
- locating examples of letters and high-frequency words in shared texts.

PRACTICAL TASK

Consider the support strategies above to help readers and choose one from each section. Devise a short practical task for each that you could use to implement these.

In view of Myers and Burnett's (2004) findings on how the lack of phonic skills can cause children to have reading difficulties, the Rose Review (DfES, 2006) also acknowledged and analysed that high-quality phonics teaching was needed to help children make progress in their reading. This was highlighted in aspect 3 of their findings.

The Rose Review (DfES, 2006) recommends that synthetic phonics teaching forms the basis of early literacy teaching. The resources used should accommodate a range of learning styles to meet the needs of all children in order for them to access the phonics programme. There should be intervention programmes in place to support children who are experiencing difficulties with reading. In the review (cited in Litterick, 2006), Rose refers to the 'three waves', which the *SEN Code of Practice* (2001) describes as a 'graduated response' to identifying and meeting SEN, and relates them to teaching and intervention to support children with significant literacy difficulties.

Wave 1 The effective inclusion of all children in daily, 'quality-first teaching'.

Wave 2 Additional intervention to enable children to work at age-related expectations or above.

Wave 3 Additional, highly personalised interventions, for example specifically targeted approaches for children identified as requiring SEN support (on School Action, School Action Plus or with a statement of SEN).

(adapted from DfES, 2006, para. 133) | 117

Brooks (2002) researched the effectiveness of intervention schemes. He published the findings in his report *What Works for Children with Literacy Difficulties*. The majority of the intervention schemes he researched were 'wave 3' programmes, although some were being used at the 'wave 2' stage. This involved analysing 25 different schemes, as he found many local authorities were using dissimilar programmes. Examples of these include: 'Better Reading Partnership', originally developed in Bradford; 'Reading Recovery', which is being used in many local authorities across the UK; the 'Knowsley Reading Project'; and 'Paired Reading' in Kirklees. He analysed how effective these schemes were in helping children to progress with their reading. The examples above found that children made progress with their reading after taking part in the intervention programmes.

REFLECTIVE TASK

Think about your setting. What intervention programmes are in place to help children with reading difficulties? How do you measure their progress?

CHAPTER SUMMARY

- There are many different theories and practice concerned with the development of reading.
- The Rose Review brought about changes to phonics teaching, early literacy teaching and early reading.
- There are many intervention programmes in place across the UK to help children with reading difficulties.

REFERENCES

Adams, M.J. (1990) *Beginning to Read: Thinking and learning about print*. Cambridge, MA: MIT Press.

Augur, J. and Briggs, S. (1992) *Hickey Multi-Sensory Language Course*. London: Whurr Publishers Ltd.

Brooks, G. (2002) *What Works for Children with Literacy Difficulties*. London: DfES. Available online at www.dcsf.gov.uk/research/data/uploadfiles/RR380.pdf (accessed 14 September 2008).

Browne, A. (1998) *A Practical Guide to Teaching Reading in the Early Years*. London: Paul Chapman.

Browne, A. (2002) *Developing Language and Literacy 3–8*. London: Paul Chapman.

Department for Children, Schools and Families (DCSF) (2007) *Early Years Foundation Stage*. Available online at www.standards.dfes.gov.uk/eyfs/site/childdevelopment/index.htm (accessed 20 November 2008).

Department for Children, Schools and Families (DCSF) (2008) *The National Strategies: Secondary*. Available online at www.standards.dfes.gov.uk/secondary/framework/ (accessed 9 September 2008).

Department for Education and Employment (DfEE) (2000) *Curriculum Guidance for the Foundation Stage*. London: QCA.

Department for Education and Skills (DfES) (2001) *SEN Code of Practice*. Nottingham: Crown.

Department for Education and Skills (DfES) (2006) *Independent Review of the Teaching of Early Reading: Final report*. Nottingham: DfES.

Department for Education and Skills (DfES) (2007) *Letters and Sounds: Principles and practice of high quality phonics*. London: DfES.

Department of Education and Science (DES) (1975) *A Language for Life* (The Bullock Report). London: HMSO.

Hall, K. (2003) *Listening to Stephen Read: Multiple perspectives on literacy*, Milton Keynes: Open University Press.

House of Commons Education and Skills Committee (2004) *Teaching Children to Read*. London: TSO.

Johnston, R. and Watson, J. (2005) *A Seven Year Study of the Effects of Synthetic Phonics Teaching on Reading and Spelling Attainment*. Available online at www.scotland.gov.uk/Publications/2005/02/20682/52383 (accessed 30 August 2008).

Johnston, R. and Watson, J. (2007) *Teaching Synthetic Phonics*. Exeter: Learning Matters.

Lewis, M. and Ellis, S. (eds) (2006) *Phonics: Practice, research and policy*. London: Paul Chapman.

Litterick, I. (2006) *How can Technology Help with Phonics?* Available online at www.dyslexic.com/phonics (accessed 14 September 2008).

Lloyd, S. and Wernham, S. (2005) *Jolly Phonics*. Available online at www.jollylearning.co.uk/ (accessed 20 November 2008).

Myers, J. and Burnett, C. (2004) *Teaching English 3–11*. London: Continuum.

Smith, F. (1999) Why systematic phonics and phonemic awareness instruction constitute an educational hazard. *Language Arts*, 77(2): 150–5.

Snowling, M.J. and Hulme, C. (eds) (2007) *The Science of Reading: A handbook*. Oxford: Blackwell.

FURTHER READING

Johnston, R. and Watson, J. (2007) *Teaching Synthetic Phonics*. Exeter: Learning Matters.

Lewis, M. and Ellis, S. (eds) (2006) *Phonics: Practice, research and policy*. London: Paul Chapman.

Mallett, M. (2008) *The Primary English Encyclopedia: The heart of the curriculum edition: 3*. London: Routledge.

10 CURRICULUM ENRICHMENT THROUGH *EXCELLENCE AND ENJOYMENT*

Elizabeth Kirtlan

CHAPTER OBJECTIVES

By the end of this chapter you will:

- understand the significance of the DfES *Excellence and Enjoyment: A strategy for primary schools* (2003) for the foundation subjects curriculum and its management;

- be aware of theory relating to the holistic curriculum and motivation theory;

- be aware of the role of support staff through this strategy.

LINKS TO **HLTA** STANDARDS

1. Have high expectations of children and young people with a commitment to helping them fulfil their potential.

2. Improve their own knowledge and practice, including responding to advice and feedback.

3. Know how to contribute to effective personalised provision by taking practical account of diversity.

4. Have sufficient understanding of their area(s) of expertise to support the development, learning and progress of children and young people.

5. Know how statutory and non-statutory frameworks for the school curriculum relate to the age and ability ranges of the learners they support.

6. Know how other frameworks, which support the development and well-being of children and young people, impact upon your practice.

7. Devise clearly structured activities that interest and motivate learners and advance their learning.

Introduction

This chapter looks at the significance of the DfES *Excellence and Enjoyment: A strategy for primary schools* (2003) for the foundation subjects curriculum and its management. It will examine the underpinning theory related to the holistic curriculum and motivation theory and the role of support staff. Terms such as 'enrichment' will be considered through case studies.

Foundation subjects

In 1988, the Education Reform Act was introduced (OPSI, 2008). This act was to change teaching in schools dramatically and, within it, the National Curriculum was introduced. The following aspects were highlighted.

- The government sanctioned a common curriculum for pupils aged 5–16.
- There was a shift in responsibility away from teachers and towards central government for what was to be taught. Previously, teachers worked out schemes of work that were deemed appropriate for their pupils.
- Three core subjects and seven foundation subjects were introduced at the primary phase. For secondary pupils, a modern foreign language was to be taught in addition to these. The foundation subjects were art, design and technology, geography, history, music and physical education (PE). The act stated that each subject would comprise:
  - attainment targets: the knowledge, skills and understanding that pupils of different abilities and maturities are expected to have by the end of each key stage;
  - programmes of study: the matters, skills and processes that are required to be taught to pupils of different abilities and maturities during each key stage;
  - assessment arrangements: the arrangements for assessing pupils at or near the end of each key stage for the purpose of ascertaining what they have achieved in relation to the attainment targets for that stage.

No longer, then, could schools and teachers deliver what they wanted, as had been the case prior to the Reform Act. Schools and teachers had not been subject to any national prescription concerning curricula, pedagogy and teaching method requirements (except for PE and RE), as these were viewed as the product of professional judgement (McCulloch et al., cited in Webb, 2006). The foundation subjects, therefore, were being taught as single subjects within the curriculum in many schools for the first time. This curriculum was revised between 1998 and 1999 under New Labour, with the introduction of the National Literacy Strategy (NLS) and the National Numeracy Strategy (NNS). A revised National Curriculum document was released in 2000, which is still statutory today.

> **PRACTICAL TASK**
> In your school settings, find out how the foundation subjects are delivered? Have changes been made to the delivery of these? How?

Excellence and Enjoyment: A strategy for primary schools

In May 2003, the Secretary of State for Education and Skills, Charles Clarke, launched *Excellence and Enjoyment: A strategy for primary schools*. He stated:

> *I believe that what makes good primary education great is the fusion of excellence and enjoyment. Excellent teaching gives children the life chance they deserve . . . Enjoyment is the birthright of every child.*
>
> (DfES, 2003, p1)

He went on to say:

> *But the most powerful mix is the one that brings the two together. Children learn better when they are excited and engaged – but what excites and engages them best is truly excellent teaching, which challenges them and shows them what they can do. When there is joy in what they are doing, they learn to love learning.*
>
> (ibid.)

The importance of the strategy, he felt, was that:

> *Different schools [will] go about this in different ways. There will be different sparks that make learning vivid and real for different children. I want every primary school to be able to build on their own strengths to serve the needs of their own children. To do this, they will work with parents and the whole community; they will think creatively about how they use the skills of everyone in the school.*
>
> (ibid.)

The strategy outlines aims for what schools should do to combine high standards with a broad and rich curriculum, as follows.

- **Develop the distinctive character of their school** – by, for example, developing strengths in sport or music or special needs, or working very closely with the local community.
- **Take ownership of the curriculum** – by shaping it and making it their own. Teachers have much more freedom than they often realise to design the timetable and decide what and how they teach.
- **Be creative and innovative** – in how they teach and run the school.
- **Use tests, targets and tables to help every child** – to develop to his or her potential, help the school to improve and help parents and the public to understand the progress of the pupils and the performance of the school.

This is what many schools are doing. Barnes (2007, p129) notes how schools have taken a more flexible approach to their curriculum and have moved away from the rigid interpretation of the NLS and the NNS, using 'thinking partners', group investigations, problem solving and role play. Making links with other subjects and with practical situations is now more common. This change of style takes account of the different school and cultural contexts, the various styles of thinking and learning, the multiple emotional needs and also a variety of ways of showing intelligence.

The strategy also highlights creativity as the main focus of enriching the curriculum. QCA materials, *Creativity: Find it, promote it* (2003), have been developed as part of the strategy, and are the outcome of a three-year project working with 120 teachers. The QCA asked these teachers to investigate how they could develop their pupils' creativity through their existing schemes of work and lesson plans. This was across all national curriculum subjects at Key Stages 1–3. The materials look at how promoting pupils' creativity can:

- improve pupils' self-esteem, motivation and achievement;
- develop skills for adult life;
- develop the talent of the individual.

Taking the terms 'creativity' and 'enrichment', the next section will examine theories in teaching the curriculum through *Excellence and Enjoyment*.

Underpinning theory related to the holistic curriculum and motivation theory

There are many theories relating to the holistic curriculum and motivation theory. They consider why children learn and what motivates them to learn. Teachers can draw upon these theories to help them determine how to enrich the curriculum and how to be creative with it.

What is motivation?

Motivation can be termed as the internal desire or drive to undertake some behaviour or action. There are other contextual factors that enable successful learning, such as behaviour management, parental aspirations and personal aspirations. Motivation theory refers to lots of different theories to explain what motivates people. There needs to be a goal and then there needs to be a driving force to achieve the goal, but which comes first? The need to achieve, or the goal?

Broadly speaking, then, motivation is either *intrinsic/expressive* (doing something for its own sake) or *extrinsic/ instrumental* (doing something for some other reason). A useful, slightly more detailed, categorisation is shown in the table on page 124 (based on Atherton, 2005).

What motivates pupils to learn?

- Intrinsically – curiosity, interest, power, self-worth, internal drive to self-actualise.
- Extrinsically – rewards: verbal praise, stickers, free play time, etc.; fear of punishment/ sanctions, wanting to please teacher.

REFLECTIVE TASK
Which one of the categories above would you place yourself in at this moment? Does motivation type and level depend on the task? Now think of children. Does their motivation vary on the task they are to undertake and, if so, why? What influences this?

	INTRINSIC		EXTRINSIC	
	EXPRESSIVE	ACHIEVEMENT	SOCIAL	INSTRUMENTAL
Characteristics	Interest for its own sake: satisfaction derived directly from understanding/skill.	Desire to succeed: 'I'm not going to let this beat me': mastery represents something important.	In order to gain social acceptance, either within the class/course, etc.: 'pleasing teacher' or being one of the in-crowd.	In order to gain a tangible reward or avoid negative consequences.
Strengths	Enthusiasm, commitment.	Commitment.	Co-operativeness if class-oriented.	Can develop into more significant commitment.
Weaknesses	May get 'carried away': lose sight of wood for trees.	Potentially fickle. What the learning represents to the student may not be the same as what it represents to you.	May concentrate on the appearance of achievement to the detriment of 'deep' learning. Social aspirations may change.	Achievement rests on strict criteria of 'relevance'. Aspirations may be met in other ways. Anxiety may impede learning.

Motivation by needs

Abraham Maslow developed the Hierarchy of Needs model in the USA in the 1940s–1950s, and the theory remains valid today for understanding human motivation and personal development. Maslow's Hierarchy of Needs is a 'content theory' of motivation.

Each of us is motivated by needs. Our most basic needs are inborn, having evolved over tens of thousands of years. Maslow's Hierarchy of Needs helps to explain how these needs motivate us all, and it states that we must satisfy each need in turn, starting with the first, which deals with the most obvious needs for survival itself. When the lower-order needs of physical and emotional well-being are satisfied, we then move up and concern ourselves with the higher-order needs of influence and personal development. Equally, if the things that satisfy our lower-order needs are swept away, we are no longer concerned about the maintenance of our higher-order needs (Maslow, 1954).

In Maslow's concept of self-actualisation, he notes that people who are at this stage have many characteristics, one of them being 'creative' (Craft, 2006). According to Maslow, motivation also occurs when children/adults are at the self-actualisation stage.

Lev Vygotsky (cited in Mooney, 2000) stated that we learn a lot from each other and our surroundings; schools have the 'hidden curriculum', so children receive motivation and encouragement in their learning from other people.

However, learning is not as straightforward as this, as it will change with interventions and the social contexts of learning.

REFLECTIVE TASK

Consider these questions in relation to motivation and the pupils in your settings.

* How do schools, teachers and TAs motivate children to learn?
* What demotivates pupils in your experience?
* How do you overcome poor motivation?
* What in the current system of education inhibits pupil motivation?
* What encourages self-motivation?
* Consider the impact of classroom organisation on the motivation of pupils in the learning process.

Facilitating learning through motivation theory

One of the key theories relating to motivation is holistic theory. It argues that motivation relates to the fact that the *individual personality consists of many elements . . . specifically . . . the intellect, emotions, the body impulse (or desire), intuition and imagination* (Laird, 1985, p121). All require activation if learning is to be more effective.

Carl Rogers and others have developed the theory of facilitative learning. The background behind this theory is that learning will occur by the educator acting as a facilitator, by establishing an atmosphere in which learners feel comfortable to consider new ideas and are not threatened by external factors (Laird, 1985, cited in Dunn, 2000). Another characteristic of this theory is that humans have a natural eagerness to learn.

Within this theory, learners:

- are encouraged to take responsibility for their own learning;
- provide much of the input for the learning, which occurs through their insights and experiences;
- are encouraged to consider that the most valuable evaluation is self-evaluation and that learning needs to focus on factors that contribute to solving significant problems or achieving significant results.

Through teaching this way, children are developing new skills and taking responsibility for their learning, thus creating a sense of achievement in return. This supports motivation theory; if children are feeling motivated to want to learn, and are forming a natural curiosity about the topics, they are learning. This is reflected in the case studies in the next section.

Case studies

This section of the chapter is dedicated to examining case studies around *Excellence and Enjoyment* (DfES, 2003). It shows how schools have taken different aspects of the strategy and have begun to implement these within their school settings, by making changes to their curriculum to enhance children's learning and experiences.

The first case study is from a school in Bolton, which has changed its curriculum in line with the strategy.

CASE STUDY 1

All Saints Primary School is situated on the outskirts of Bolton; it has over 200 children on roll with a high percentage of children from ethnic minority backgrounds. In 2005, the head teacher formed a 'Creative Curriculum' working party. This comprised teachers from Key Stages 1 and 2 and the senior leadership team. Over a number of weeks, the staff met to discuss their existing curriculum, considering what worked well and what could be changed to benefit the children and staff. The school was currently using the QCA schemes of work. Some were excellent and others, they felt, didn't really meet the needs of the children, so this was their starting point.

Through discussions with staff and co-ordinators in staff meetings, the working party developed long-term plans for the whole school based on a thematic approach. In Key Stage 1, there was to be a new topic every half term, as it was felt that the children would not be able to focus on the theme for any longer. Key Stage 2 had three themes, one for each term. They decided that the themes would cover geography, history and science-based topics. Mind maps were drawn up to illustrate the cross-curricular links that could be made. If subjects could not be linked to the theme, the subject would be taught alone.

The change in curriculum has now been running for three years. The school has seen changes in the children's attainment and it is evident that their enjoyment in school is making a significant contribution towards their learning.

REFLECTIVE TASK
Looking at case study 1, think about the challenges that faced the school in changing the curriculum in this way. What advantages are there to forming a creative curriculum?

The next case study examines how health and the use of energy, transport and school grounds combine to enrich the curriculum as the school focuses on *Excellence and Enjoyment*.

CASE STUDY 2

A primary school in the North West of England has 234 children aged between 4 and 11 on roll. The school is in a socially deprived area and has 60 per cent of children with English as an additional language.

Outline of the project
Responsibility for sustainable development is largely shared between three members of staff. The head teacher and governing body support the work in school to ensure smooth running of the project.

Practice: curriculum
- *Sustainable development features in the curriculum largely through geography, with links made to other subjects as appropriate.*
- *The children are involved in many projects within the curriculum including cookery, gardening clubs and improving the school grounds and the locality.*

Practice: decision making
The school has an eco team, which meets weekly. It is chaired by a senior teacher and includes representatives from each class. The team regularly focuses on global sustainability issues and issues affecting the local community.

Energy and water
- *Monitors check classrooms to ensure that lights are switched off, computers are not left on and that taps no longer drip.*

Waste
- *The school recycles waste paper, tins and cardboard recycling scheme.*
- *Garden waste, leaves and garden waste are collected in the school compost bins.*
- *Children collect litter on the school site.*

Travel and traffic
The school is in the process of drawing up a school travel plan, with the help of the local authority and they participated in the international walk-to-school week. The school awards the class with the highest percentage of walkers a trophy every week.

The school grounds
- *The school is developing a wide range of habitats. It has extensive grounds and is endeavouring to create habitats for wild flowers, insects and birds as well as creating flower gardens and vegetable plots.*

- *The school has a gardening club that meets every Friday lunchtime and more regularly during the summer months. Last year the vegetables they grew were used in cooking and sold at a summer fair.*

Food and drink
The school has focused on healthy eating and has engaged in a programme of encouraging healthy snacks with rewards and certificates for children taking part. In addition to this the school has achieved 'active mark' as a result of improved provision for PE. The school also encourages fitness and has invited a number of outside agency coaches into school to promote this.

Timings and activities
The school has begun to cultivate links with a local recycling plant and a visit to the plant is planned in the near future. Activities are mostly undertaken in class time or at lunchtimes. The school has devoted a professional development day to improving and using the school grounds.

Challenges
- *Time and money. The school holds regular events to raise funds to continue to improve the grounds.*

What's next?
- *Development of the school travel plan.*
- *Possible development of the 'Walk on Wednesday' scheme to include extra days or even a walking bus.*

REFLECTIVE TASK

Think about your setting and case study 2. What changes are being made around the issues of health and the use of energy, transport and school grounds?

This final case study draws on how teachers are using the *Excellence and Enjoyment* strategy in their classrooms. It looks at a cross-curricular week for Year 6 children, set around features in the local country park.

CASE STUDY 3

Children in Year 6 were invited by the rangers at the local country park to take part in a week-long cross-curricular study. The activities were designed in consultation with staff to bring both nature and the curriculum to life.

The activities included:
- *art;*
- *science;*
- *geography;*
- *PE;*
- *mathematics;*
- *literacy.*

During the week, children participated in these activities and were grouped in mixed ability groups working on a carousel basis. In the art workshop children designed their own clay stones to go in a special area of the park. The stones had to symbolise an animal or plant in the park.

The science workshop looked at adaptation and interdependence of the wildlife within the park. The children collected specimens, examined plants and looked at food chains within the park. Linking with the science workshop, in geography they studied the migratory birds that visit the country park every year. In the park's classroom, the children looked at the countries these birds had come from and the journeys they had made.

Taking one animal that lives in the park, the children completed orienteering activities modelling the range that the animal might have, for example a fox. Using given information from rangers' records, in mathematics, children worked out potential numbers of animals in the park and estimated for future years. This included using range data-handling skills to produce charts and tables. Lastly, in literacy, children could choose from a range of activities to portray their time in the park – these ranged from recounts to poems.

Teachers and support staff worked in different workshops to support and guide children in the activities. They assisted with questioning the children to develop their thinking. Following the week's activities, arrangements were made for a follow-up visit by rangers to the school; again the importance of support staff was vital in helping children to recall activities.

REFLECTIVE TASK

- Are there cross-curricular themes similar to those in case study 3 being taught in your setting? How are they being taught? Discuss with colleagues in school.
- The case study mentioned support staff being involved in the activities. Have you been involved in cross-curricular themes? What was your role?

The final section of this chapter will be examining the role of support staff in the creative curriculum.

The role of support staff

The role of support staff is very important in supporting pupils' learning through a 'creative curriculum'. TAs can support pupils individually or support whole classes by co-ordinating projects. The TA can give guidance to ensure they make progress and begin their independent learning journey. According to Watkinson:

If we can see the potential learning of pupils we can put in place stepping stones or 'scaffolding' to bring them to the next stage of development – a clear role for a perceptive TA . . . The important thing for the pupil is that the TAs provide the scaffolding, not build the complete tower.

(2003, p66)

The process of scaffolding does not limit the development of creative thought in pupils; rather, it can promote creative thinking through the use of open-ended questioning. Other strategies to develop creative thought are provided by the QCA materials, *Creativity: Find it, promote it* (2003). These can be summarised as follows.

- Actively encourage pupils to question, make connections, envisage what might be and explore ideas. Promote and reward imagination and originality.
- Ask open-ended questions, such as 'What if . . .?' and 'How might you . . .?' to help pupils see things from different perspectives.
- Value and praise what pupils do and say. Establish an atmosphere in which they feel safe to say things, take risks and respond creatively.
- Create a fun, relaxed working environment if you want to encourage pupils to be adventurous and explore ideas freely.
- Create conditions for quiet reflection and concentration if you want to encourage pupils to work imaginatively.
- Make the most of unexpected events. When appropriate, put aside your lesson plan and 'go with the moment', but never lose sight of your overall learning objectives.
- Be willing to stand back and let pupils take the lead. However, make sure that you are always on hand to provide prompts and support as needed.
- Join in with activities and model creative thinking and behaviour. Showing the pupils that you are a learner too can help to create an open, constructive learning environment.

REFLECTIVE TASK

Look over the pointers again; think about your role in your setting. How do you promote creativity? Do you do any of the above? Think about how you fulfil these.

CHAPTER SUMMARY

- The DfES *Excellence and Enjoyment: A strategy for primary schools* (2003) has great significance for the foundation subjects curriculum and its management.
- There are many theories relating to the holistic curriculum and motivation theory, and teachers can draw upon these theories to enrich the curriculum and enhance creativity.
- Schools have implemented the strategy in many different ways, by making changes to their curriculum to enhance pupils' learning and experiences.
- Support staff have an important role in supporting and developing the *Excellence and Enjoyment* strategy.

REFERENCES

Atherton, J.S. (2005) *Learning and Teaching: Motivation.* Available online at www.learningandteaching.info/learning/motivation.htm (accessed 9 October 2008).

Barnes, J. (2007) *Cross-Curricular Learning 3–14.* London: Paul Chapman.

Craft, A. (2006) *Creativity across the Primary Curriculum.* London, Routledge.

Department for Education and Skills (DfES) (2003) *Excellence and Enjoyment: A strategy for primary schools.* London: DfES.

Dunn, S. (2000) *Theories of Learning*. Oxford Brookes University. Available online at
www.brookes.ac.uk/services/ocsd/2_learntch/theories.html#holistic (accessed
1 October 2008).

Laird, D. (1985) Approaches to training and development, in Dunn, S. (2000) *Theories of
Learning*. Oxford: Oxford Brookes University. Available online at www.brookes.ac.uk/
services/ocsd/2_learntch/theories.html#holistic (accessed 1 October 2008).

Maslow, A. (1954) Motivation and personality, in *Maslow's Hierarchy of Needs* (2nd edn, 1970).
Available online at www.businessballs.com/maslow.htm (accessed 9 October 2008).

Mooney, C. (2000) *Theories of Childhood*, St Paul, MN: Red Leaf Press.

Office of Public Sector Information (OPSI) (2008) *Education Reform Act (1988)*. Available online
at www.opsi.gov.uk/acts/acts1988/ukpga_19880040_en_2#pt1-ch1-pb1-l1g1 (accessed
17 October 2008).

Qualifications and Curriculum Authority (QCA) (2000) *National Curriculum*. London: HMSO.

Qualifications and Curriculum Authority (QCA) (2003) *Creativity: Find it, promote it*. Available
online at http://curriculum.qca.org.uk/key-stages-1-and-2/learning-across-the-curriculum/
creativity/index.aspx (accessed 5 October 2008).

teachernet (n.d.) *Case Studies*. Available online at www.teachernet.gov.uk/CaseStudies/
casestudy.cfm?id=552 (accessed 23 September 2008).

Watkinson, A. (2003) *The Essential Guide for Experienced Teaching Assistants*. London: Fulton.

Webb, R. (2006) *Changing Teaching and Learning in the Primary School*. Buckingham: Open
University Press.

FURTHER READING

Barnes, J. (2007) *Cross-Curricular Learning 3–14*. London: Paul Chapman.

Craft, A. (2006) *Creativity across the Primary Curriculum*. London: Routledge.

11 IMPLEMENTING THE 14–19 CURRICULUM

Vicky Duckworth and Sue Farrimond

CHAPTER OBJECTIVES

By the end of this chapter you will:

- recognise and understand the social and economic drives that have impacted upon the 14–19 curriculum.
- understand the motivational factors that support young people, their learning and training goals.
- recognise how teaching assistants (TAs) can provide holistic support for young people through the 14–19 transition period.
- explore how TAs can empower young people to reach their potential and make a worthwhile contribution to society.

LINKS TO **HLTA** STANDARDS

This chapter addresses the majority of standards; however, there are clear and explicit links to the following.

1. Have high expectations of children and young people with a commitment to helping them fulfil their potential.

2. Establish fair, respectful, trusting, supportive and constructive relationships with children and young people.

3. Recognise and respect the contribution that parents and carers can make to the development and well-being of children and young people.

4. Know how to contribute to effective personalised provision by taking practical account of diversity.

5. Know how other frameworks, which support the development and well-being of children and young people, impact upon their practice.

6. Devise clearly structured activities that interest and motivate learners and advance their learning.

7. Plan how they will support the inclusion of the children and young people in learning activities.

8. Contribute to the selection and preparation of resources suitable for children's and young people's interests and abilities.

Introduction

This chapter will focus on the initiative to increase motivation and achievement in the secondary and further education (FE) settings. It will also examine the government's strategy to reduce the number of NEETs (not in employment, education or training) and to ensure that all young people are provided with quality learning and training opportunities. It will provide you with a knowledge of the research evidence and social and economic drivers that led to this reform. You will be able to consider how your intervention can support and empower a range of learners through practical and reflective activities. This chapter draws on the social practice model based on New Literacy Studies (Barton and Hamilton, 2000), which looks at people's literacy practices in their everyday lives.

Political and social drivers

Overview

In order for the UK to succeed and compete in the globalised economy, it is clear that young people need to possess skills that combine the theoretical with the practical and recognise that both have equal status. This will facilitate possession of a wider range of experience built into a holistic curriculum, which motivates learners to engage in lifelong learning. With the school-leaving age rising to 18, it is essential that school leavers of the future have qualifications and skills that will set them on the right path to active engagement within the workforce.

The government's drive to meet these future needs resulted in the reform of 14–19 education, which in turn has led to the introduction of Diplomas. New Diplomas will not replace existing qualifications such as GCSEs, A levels, NVQs and apprenticeships, but will be offered alongside these qualifications to help ensure that all young people can access training and education that are tailored to their individual needs. It is highly likely, for example, that a Key Stage 4 learner would study a Diploma together with a range of GCSEs.

Diplomas are by nature more practice-oriented, with schools, FE colleges and employers working together to provide suitable resources, learning environments and support for each learner to actively and successfully partake in their chosen route. As such, learners spend time in an environment more like a workplace, such as a workshop; they may also be offered the opportunity to work with an employer. The government's aim is to pull together the divide between the academic and practical routes and, in so doing, raise the status of the vocational pathways for employability and generate responsive citizenship.

Diplomas will be introduced in a phased way according to the schedule overleaf.

The participation in Diplomas is flexible and can be adapted to suit the learner's needs; for example, consider these three routes.

- Full-time over two years.
- Part-time in conjunction with employment.
- Foundation or Higher Diploma taken at age 16 or over (generally completed in a shorter period of time).

PHASE	LINE OF LEARNING	AVAILABILITY
Phase 1	IT Engineering Construction and the built environment Society, health and development Creative and media	September 2008
Phase 2	Environmental and land-based studies Manufacturing and product design Hospitality and catering Health and beauty Business, administration and finance	September 2009
Phase 3	Travel and tourism Public services Retail Sport and leisure	September 2010

Similarly, the routes are also flexible.

- University – Advanced Diploma is equivalent to three A levels.
- Employment – the Diplomas can equip learners with the skills and knowledge for their occupational trajectories.

The journey so far . . .

It is important to recognise and understand the historical development of education and training in Britain. If we rewind education practice, and indeed society, to 50 years ago, personalisation of learning was generally limited to streaming and setting. Consider the eleven-plus examination, which categorised learners into specific institutions, such as grammar or secondary modern schools, with a perceived predestined future for these learners. Galloway et al. clearly explain how this education system satisfied the social and economic situation:

> *It was of no immediate importance to industry, nor to the country's economy, that Britain was producing a higher proportion of unqualified school leavers than any of our competitor countries in Europe.*

> (1998, p13)

For years, the idea that intelligence and learning could be developed, and that skills and the ability to learn independently were more important than the acquisition and regurgitation of knowledge, hardly existed in our culture. As Gilbert clearly states:

> *How many people have had their life blighted – written off even – by the idea of not being very intelligent but being 'good with their hands'? How much genius and richness of human potential has been denied us by a system that has so very narrow a view of intelligence?*

> (2003, p43)

More recently, the drive for measured value added, publication of league tables and the introduction of the National Curriculum has focused education on to a narrow range of academic results. Teachers who previously ensured that the curriculum would interest the learner are now given a compulsory syllabus. A substantial amount of importance has been placed upon schools' external examination results to the detriment of the development of the whole learner. Moore summarises the impact of the National Curriculum as *A rapid and heavy increase in a very narrow but very high stakes system of national testing* (2006, p1).

Many schools have now reached an operational ceiling in terms of attainment and the government is concerned. Yet, we still have close to 10 per cent of young people in neither employment nor training (DCSF, 2008). If the government is genuinely committed to personalised learning, the process needs to be applied to the complete experience of learning, including curriculum and assessment.

The introduction of vocational qualifications is aimed at bridging the gap between school and FE and training. The drive was to attract pupils who would normally be deterred from continuing in some form of post-compulsory education at 16, an imperative that has strengthened now that the decision has been made to raise the compulsory school-leaving age to 18. The Diplomas are to be delivered by consortia, typically a large college of FE, with a number of local schools linked in. Further to this, each of the Diplomas needs to have cemented formal links with employers, who help with the design and delivery of them. This will mean finding new effective models of teaching and learning that build on best practice. Factors that contribute to this will be the timetabling of students across different sites, such as college, school and workplace, and an effective collaboration in curriculum design that will address functional and vocational skills in a meaningful way.

The impact of policy

A number of key policies have been integral to the development of the Diplomas.

The 14–19 white paper

The new Diplomas were developed following a government-led enquiry into 14–19 education, headed by former schools inspector, Sir Mike Tomlinson. The result of this enquiry was a 14–19 Education and Skills white paper, published in February 2005, which set out proposals that build on the strengths of the existing education system. According to the DCSF, they were designed to:

Ensure that every young person masters functional English and maths before they leave education *The reforms place renewed emphasis on the basics throughout the secondary phase, putting achievement in English and maths at the heart of new general (GCSE) Diplomas and specialised Diplomas.*

Improve vocational education *The proposals introduce new specialised lines of learning leading to Diplomas in 14 broad sector areas. Employers, through Sector Skills Councils, will lead in their design and higher education institutions will also have an important role to play. The specialised Diplomas will replace the current system of around 3,500 separate qualifications and will provide an alternative gateway to higher education and skilled employment.*

Stretch all young people and help universities to differentiate between the best candidates The reforms will free up the curriculum at Key Stages 3 and 4 to give time for stretch. Where students are able to take qualifications early they should do, and schools and colleges will get recognition for supporting them.

At advanced level, stretch will be secured by the introduction, after piloting, of more demanding, optional questions at A level and an extended project, and the availability of HE modules. Universities will get information about candidates' unit grades.

Remotivate disengaged learners The proposals will ensure that these students have extra support to master the basics, have more choice over where to learn, and can benefit from a new programme for 14–16 year olds, based on Entry to Employment. A new level 1 Diploma will provide progression.

Ensure delivery The white paper sets out a national entitlement of a full range of GCSEs, A levels and 14 specialised Diplomas. In each area of the country a prospectus will set out the courses available locally.

(DCSF, 2008)

The Leitch Review

The Leitch Review was established in 2004 to consider the UK's long-term skills needs in order to maximise economic growth, productivity and social justice within the context of the rapidly changing global economy. Its remit was to focus on adult skills. This is because 70 per cent of the 2020 working population has already left compulsory education. In July 2007, Lord Leitch published his final report, *Prosperity for All in the Global Economy: World class skills*. This examined the UK's long-term skills needs and set out ambitious goals for 2020, which, if achieved, would make the UK a world leader in skills.

It recommends radical change across the whole skills spectrum by:

- *increasing skill attainments at all levels;*
- *routing public funding of vocational skills through Train to Gain and Learner accounts;*
- *strengthening the employer voice on skills through creation of a new Commission for Employment and Skills, increasing employer engagement and investment in skills, and reforming Sector Skills Councils who will simplify and approve vocational training;*
- *launching a new 'pledge' for employers to voluntarily train more employees at work; if insufficient progress has been made by 2010, introduce a statutory right for employees to access workplace training;*
- *increasing employer investment in higher level qualifications, especially in Apprenticeships and in degree and postgraduate levels; significantly more training in the workplace;*
- *raising people's aspirations and awareness of the value of skills, creating a new universal adult careers service to diagnose skill needs with a skills health check available for all;*
- *government introducing compulsory education or workplace training up to age 18 following introduction of new Diplomas and expanded apprenticeship route; and*
- *integrating the public employment and skills services to deliver sustainable employment, enabling more disadvantaged people to gain skills and find work, developing employer-led Employment and Skills Boards.*

(Leitch Review of Skills, 2006)

Motivating 14–19-year-old learners

The ability to motivate all learners is crucial; often our learners *can seem incredibly motivated not to be motivated* (Long, 2005, p1). Most of us want to contribute to society and continually improve ourselves in ways that are personal to us; we can be motivated by financial gain, recognition, passion or intrigue, to name but a few. What is crucial is that practitioners must understand their learners, their culture and what it is that motivates them. We also need to understand why students might lack motivation and whether they have continually faced failure. Do they fear failure and, therefore, avoid it, together with any hope of academic success? If we fail to reform, many young people will continue to be disaffected with education and carve out their own measured success (Marsh, 1990; Galloway et al., 1998). It is also vital to recognise the barriers to learning that students face. One such barrier may be that learners have experienced violence or trauma in the public and/or private domain. Providing a holistic programme that recognises and addresses all a pupil's needs is vital if meaningful learning is to take place (Horsman,1999).

REFLECTIVE TASK

Consider your own experience of education and/or employment and training between the ages of 14 and 19.

- What subjects did you choose to study?
- What influenced these choices?
- How did your feel while studying these?
- Did you feel motivated?

Reflect on what has demotivated and motivated you throughout your own learning and training journey and identify strategies that would have helped you to be more motivated.

Strategies

In what ways do your strategies match with the suggestions below?

- Holistic and personalised approaches.
- Recognition of different learning styles and matching learning activities to these.
- Screening and diagnostics on entry to programme to identify areas for development.
- Realistic target setting.

The changing role of the teaching assistant

In line with the recent reforms in the school workforce, TAs are expanding their role, from classroom support to organising and supervising many of the off-site courses and supporting individual pupils with option and career choices. If you work in secondary settings, undertake the following task.

REFLECTIVE TASK
- Think of the changes to the 14–19 frameworks; what effect have they had on your role, or might they have in the future?
- Discuss this with your colleagues and evaluate the effectiveness of your possible involvement with the 14–19 curriculum to ensure pupil success.

PRACTICAL TASK

TAs frequently work with some of the most vulnerable, troubled and challenging students. To test your knowledge of possibilities, consider the following pupils, each of whom has come to you for advice. Create proposed learning journeys for the young people in the boxes below.

Mark is 14 and wants to be a car mechanic. He would also like to gain his maths and English GCSEs.

Mark's possible learning journey

Charlotte is 16 and would like to be a nursery nurse. She has level 1 in literacy and numeracy.

Charlotte's possible learning journey

Graham is just 18 and would like to be a chef. He left school without any qualifications and recently returned to learning at the local FE college.

Graham's possible learning journey

Challenges

Some of the challenges facing school support staff involved in this new curriculum focus on the following key needs.

- Individualised learning.
- Promoting independent learning.
- Working with employers and professionals outside the school setting.
- Identifying smart and realistic goals for the learners.
- Ensuring that their language, literacy, numeracy and ICT skills are being met.
- A social practice view of literacies – this offers a powerful way of conceptualising the link between the activities of reading and writing and the social structures in which they are embedded and that they help shape.

(adapted from Barton, 2006)

CASE STUDY 1

Sam is 14 and is very disruptive in English lessons. He says that they are boring and that he can't do the work. When the teacher is giving instructions he distracts the other young people when they are trying to listen. He states, 'What has all this poetry got to do with my life? It's boring.'

In response to the task above, you could offer Sam a socially situated model of literacy (Barton and Hamilton, 2000). To do this, find out what Sam is good at and enjoys doing, e.g. football, painting, music. Ask Sam to bring something to class that is important to him to create a resource to instigate literacies.

Activity	Literacies
e.g. Shopping	Reading skills, numeracy, listening, comparing

It may be a beneficial to embark on an activity that can allow the TA to engage with Sam in a holistic manner while focusing on his strengths and abilities. It will allow him to recognise and value what he can do and also let you, as a support tutor, recognise how learning straddles all aspects of life and how we can make learning relevant for Sam. Below is an example of such an activity.

School/college-based activity – poster

✓ Encourage the pupils to create a poster from magazines, comics, newspaper images, creative writing, stories, letters, text messages and items used in everyday life – receipts from new clothes, cinema timetables, television pages, problem pages from comics, football scores, heroes, etc.

✓ The pupils can then create a self-expressive 'poster' in the form of words, symbols and images.

✓ Work with the pupils in considering the strengths and skills they already have, e.g. playing football, cooking, drawing, applying make-up in a vibrant way, a Saturday job, helping parents around the house, looking after younger siblings, texting on the phone, graffiti art, etc.

✓ Put some inspirational images on the wall, e.g: sporting heroes, women and men who have fulfilled their goals despite the odds.

✓ Circulate the room facilitating the group to focus on the question and explore their emotions relating to the images they are choosing for the poster.

✓ When the posters are completed, ask the pupils to discuss their posters with the group – this is an opportunity to share ideas on how they can move forward and put strategies in place for the steps they need to take place and who they need to contact to help them on their journey. Pupils' ideas and creativity should be celebrated.

✓ The posters and discussions can be videoed and used as tools to measure the distance travelled at the end of the course. The posters could be taken home by the pupils as motivational tools.

Inclusive curriculum models 14–19 pathways

Recognition of skills and attributes content of pupils' own lives, school, community and society at large

Individual pupils will inevitably present unique and complex situations and patterns of motivation. Supporting each pupil to choose and commit to their own learning journey needs awareness of the full range of approaches, routes and support mechanisms available. The following scenarios illustrate some of the situations and needs that can be met at secondary level. Consider what you would do to help each pupil, then read through some of the recommended actions. What could be offered in your school for these pupils?

CASE STUDY 2

Amin is a high-achieving Year 10 pupil whose curriculum is traditionally academic due to parental pressure and teacher expectation. He has recently become withdrawn and uncharacteristically quiet in class and has started to underperform and appears demotivated. During a session with you, his learning guide, Amin stated that he feels that he needs to do something of a more practical nature, as he really misses the practical subjects he studied at Key Stage 3. He really enjoys working on the local urban farm and considers that he would like a career that is practically based. He admits that he is feeling despondent and unhappy with his school curriculum as it does not meet his needs.

REFLECTIVE TASK

Looking at case study 2, what can be done to re-engage Amin? Make notes on the approaches you would use. What would be available in your school?

You may have considered the following.

- Ensure that all of Amin's enrichment curriculum is practically focused.
- Discuss the situation with Amin's parents.
- Seek immediate support to review his curriculum.
- Investigate career pathways.
- Encourage Amin to see his GCSEs as a means to attain his future aims.
- Involve Amin in taster days and interviews at a local FE college.
- Ensure that Amin's contribution to the urban farm is recognised, celebrated and accredited.
- Encourage him to lead an extra-curricular practical activity for younger learners.

Coaching and mentoring: peer support and parental involvement

> CASE STUDY 3
>
> *Jane has recently returned to education after having time off to have a baby. She is 17 and a single mum and is keen to get a career eventually that will give her and her son a better life. She dreams of going to university to study to become a paediatric nurse. She is finding balancing motherhood and her studies very difficult.*

REFLECTIVE TASK

Looking at case study 3, consider ways in which you can support Jane to plan her home study. Who else do you think could support and motivate Jane?

You may have considered the following.

- Support groups.
- Peer mentoring with someone who has had similar experiences.
- Professional role models.
- Inspirational literature (see McNamara, 2007; Duckworth, 2008).
- Childcare support and funding.
- Practical support and advice, e.g. laptop, organisational skills.

Learner participation

> CASE STUDY 4
>
> *Kathy is a Year 9 pupil who has specific educational needs – she is dyslexic and has significant literacy problems, but does, however, have excellent verbal skills. She can become despondent and frustrated with her lack of academic success. Kathy has shown excellent skills in terms of her ability to listen and support her peers; she is often found helping others to reconcile differences.*

REFLECTIVE TASK

Looking at case study 4, what can be practically done to help Kathy recognise her personal skills and feel valued?

You may have considered the following.

- Ensure that Kathy's options enable her oral skills to be assessed, e.g. performing arts.
- Give Kathy a recognised position as a leader in reconciliation within the school.
- Encourage Kathy to be involved with all aspects of pupil participation, e.g. school council, pupil learning walks, focus groups.
- Investigate relevant career pathways;
- Ensure that Kathy begins to get work-based experience in her chosen career field.

Inter-agency collaboration support mechanisms

CASE STUDY 5

Witold has recently come over from Poland; he is 18 years old and determined to become a teacher. His English is poor but improving. He is living with his parents and siblings in a deprived area in an overcrowded flat. His parents are finding it difficult to secure employment, so Witold must work in the evenings in a local take-away to bring in much-needed funds. His parents are keen for Witold to work full-time in the catering business. He has been arriving at college tired and has not been submitting assignments.

REFLECTIVE TASK

- Looking at case study 5, identify the barriers to Witold's learning.
- What strategies can be put in place to address Witold's issues?
- Who do you need to contact to support the process?

You may have considered the following strategies to support Witold's learning.

- Set targets.
- Stick to achievable goals each lesson.
- Use materials that are of interest to Witold.
- Signpost Witold to student services.
- Offer a flexible approach to the delivery of the programme, e.g. learning online.
- Signpost Witold to the employment services or careers adviser, e.g. work may be available in the day to fit around his college course.
- Make available up-to-date information on student loans, grants, bursaries or scholarships.

The future

The government is to reduce the number of existing qualifications in England as the new Diplomas are all rolled out by 2013. Applied A levels are likely to be the first to go, along with thousands of little-used vocational qualifications. BTECs and City and Guilds may be subsumed in Diplomas as the system is streamlined. The current system is over-complicated and not time- or cost-effective. According to the DCSF, of the 6,500 or so existing qualifications, 65 per cent are taken by fewer than 100 students a year. Those with very low uptakes, such as a certificate for parking attendants, are likely to go, unless there is a proven demand from students and employers.

A new Joint Advisory Committee for Qualifications Approval will decide which qualifications get public funding to be offered in schools and colleges. In order to attempt to cater for all learners in this important age bracket, a revision of the current course/qualification provision is to be undertaken. To simplify the process, the government has favoured a three-pronged structure, which involves:

- GCSEs and A-levels;
- Diplomas;
- apprenticeships.

As mentioned above, as part of the streamlining process the government has indicated that it intends to remove duplication by withdrawing applied A levels, but intends to retain vocational qualifications such as BTEC, either as stand-alone qualifications or as part of the Diploma. There is also the intention to retain alternative qualifications favoured by some higher education and employer institutions, such as the International Baccalaureate and the new Pre-U course.

REFLECTIVE TASK

You might wish to reflect with your colleagues about whether the previous system was overly complex and whether or not the introduction of Diplomas as part of the above trio of qualifications will address that problem.

- What are the likely pitfalls of this new system?
- What are the benefits of it?

Whatever your views and those of your fellow professionals, the new system will radically alter the way young people prepare for the world of work with its complex and ever-changing demands. The 14–19 curriculum offers the opportunity for some exciting and innovative approaches to vocational learning to evolve. However, unless we see a corresponding and radical shift in attitudes towards a more egalitarian acceptance of the value of vocational qualifications alongside the traditional academic ones, the government's aspirations may be dashed. Working in this field of secondary education will prove to be exciting and challenging in the future.

CHAPTER SUMMARY

- It is essential for school leavers to have the necessary qualifications and skills to compete in an increasingly globalised economy.
- To this end, the government has reformed the 14–19 curriculum and has introduced new Diplomas that are better tailored to young people's individual needs.
- It is now recognised that practice-oriented subjects have equal value to academic ones and often better equip young people for the world of work.
- The changes to the 14–19 curriculum present teachers and support staff with new challenges in motivating all pupils to reach their full potential.

REFERENCES

Barton, D. (2006) Significance of a social practice view of language, literacy and numeracy, in Hamilton, M., Hillier, Y. and Tett, L. (eds) *Adult Literacy, Numeracy and Language: Policy, practice and research*. Maidenhead: Open University Press, pp22–41.

Barton, D. and Hamilton, M. (2000) Literacy practices, in Barton, D., Hamilton, M. and Ivanic, R. (eds) *Situated Literacies: Reading and writing in context*. New York: Routledge, pp7–15.

Department for Children, Schools and Families (DCSF) (2008) *14–19 Education and Skills*. Available online at www.dcsf.gov.uk/publications/14–19educationandskills/ (accessed 21 August 2008).

Duckworth, V. (2008) *Getting Better Student Worksheets*. Warrington: Gatehouse Books.

Galloway, D., Rogers, C., Armstrong, D. and Leo, E. (1998) *Motivating the Difficult to Teach*. Harlow: Longman.

Gilbert, I. (2003) *Essential Motivation in the Classroom*. London: RoutledgeFalmer.

Horsman, J. (1999) *Too Scared to Learn: Women, violence and education*, Toronto: McGilligan Books.

Leitch Review of Skills (2006) *Prosperity for All in the Global Economy: World class skills*. Available online at www.dcsf.gov.uk/furthereducation/uploads/documents/2006–12%20 LeitchReview1.pdf (accessed 14 November 2008).

Long, R. (2005) *Motivation*. London: David Fulton.

Marsh, H.W. (1990) A multidimensional, hierarchical model of self-concept: theoretical and empirical justification. *Educational Psychology Review*, 2: 77–171.

McNamara, M. (2007) *Getting Better*. Warrington: Gatehouse Books.

Moore, A. (ed.) (2006) *Schooling, Society and Curriculum*. Abingdon: Routledge.

FURTHER READING

Heath, S. (1983) *Ways with Words: Language, life and work in communities and classrooms*. Cambridge: Cambridge University Press.

Luttrell, W. (1997) *School-smart and Mother-wise*. New York: Routledge.

Mallows, D., Chester, A. and Duckworth, V. (2008) Seeing yourself in print. *NRDC: reflect online*, 10: 26.

Steedman, C. (1998) The mother made conscious, in Woodhead, M. and McGrath, A. (eds), *Family, School and Society*. London: The Open University Press.

12 EDUCATION IN THE TWENTY-FIRST CENTURY

Gillian Goddard and Anita Walton

CHAPTER OBJECTIVES

By the end of this chapter you will:

- have reflected on the present education system as part of a developing and changing provision;
- understand the various purposes of education;
- be able to speculate about future trends and developments, including those in support staff roles;
- understand some of the key influences on education development.

LINKS TO **HLTA** STANDARDS

1. Improve their own knowledge and practice.
2. Understand the key factors that affect children's and young people's learning and progress.

Introduction

Being involved in the daily practice of education delivery, it is sometimes hard to consider that the whole nature and provision of education could change. It is not that education delivery remains unchanging year on year; you will already be familiar with continuous small-scale change with wave after wave of government-led initiatives implemented in the last few years with an almost obsessive focus on improving standards of achievement. Many of you will be at the forefront of implementing those strategies and programmes, such as the 'Wave' programmes for literacy and numeracy. Yet, in this chapter, I want you to step back and consider what is done in schools and why, in the light of your own educational experience as a child. I then want you to use your imagination to break free of the present structures and ways of doing things in education to reach into the future and speculate about the shape of schooling 20 years on.

To do this, we will need to explore what the whole point of education is and what influences its provision and objectives. In the latter half of the chapter we will focus particularly on new technologies and their impact on the world of teaching and learning. It is in this area that we have seen the greatest changes of practice.

What is education for?

There may well have been times when you have actually asked yourself the question, 'What is the point of this?' Aldrich, a social historian, wrote, rather tongue in cheek:

> The term education might be applied to the process whereby society, or state, seeks to furnish itself with wise rulers, brave warriors, holy clerics, efficient businessmen, industrious workers and domesticated womenfolk.

(1982, p35)

Think for a moment about what Aldrich is saying here. Education has always been used, whether free or paid for, to create and maintain a stable, efficient, functioning and profitable society based on the development of vocational knowledge and skills. In Aldrich's view, it also involved, and still involves, the implicit indoctrination of an individual into their vocational 'place' in that society. Do you agree with that?

PRACTICAL TASK

Write down some notes on the way your educational setting actively develops future workplace skills and knowledge. What does it do that doesn't specifically enhance the pupils' chances of getting good jobs?

For example, teaching ICT skills is likely to have a direct relevance for employment requirements, but you might consider that teaching about the Tudors in history is not directly valuable for employability.

The purposes of education

There have been other important reasons why individuals and interest groups such as employers, the Church and the state have paid for their children to be taught something.

REFLECTIVE TASK

Try to think of as many reasons as you can for educating children and write them down.

Here are some reasons taken from the last two millennia.

- **Survival in life**
  This is the most fundamental and powerful reason for teaching children. Virtually all parents and families do this and are concerned with maximising their children's chances of keeping safe. Think about what you were taught by your family that helped you to keep safe.

- **Socialisation**
  We are social beings. We are programmed to live in groups and to survive better by co-operating with one another. The length of our maturation from infant to adulthood means that we are dependent on having one or more parents or carers living with us and tending to our needs. For this biological reason we need to be taught as children how to get on with people, how to compromise, how to lead, how to follow and how to read others'

emotions and motives. Think again of how your family helped you to manage social relationships well.

- **Preparation for the workplace**

  Survival, and certainly 'getting on' in life, is largely dependent on the type of work we get. Much energy is spent and has always been spent in making children 'fit' for specific types of work. The apprenticeships of the medieval period, recently revived, were a formal expression of the need for the young (and not so young) to be given the opportunity to learn new skills associated with a particular job. You are doing that now, studying and developing your skills in the workplace.

- **Preservation of cultural values and identity**

  This has always been taught to children, whether in the family or community, or peer group or school. It is hard to define what is being taught, for values are often not explicitly taught but implicitly inculcated by dominant individuals and groups, where belonging depends on your adherence to a particular set of codes or beliefs. Indeed, your personal identity is often characterised by a set of communally held and transmitted values, given to you as children, then later acquired as part of your work. To consider what values and attitudes we encourage in school as part of our attempts at acculturation, have a look at the National Curriculum's *Statement of Values* (DfEE/QCA, 1999, pp147–9). Failing to successfully inculcate shared values creates difficulties for any society. Have you met any children whose family and community values and attitudes may be at odds with your own? I remember teaching Year 6 pupils in my first teaching practice when I was training to be a teacher. The school was in one of the most deprived areas of Liverpool. I urged the pupils to work hard at their maths and English so that they could get good jobs when they grew up. Most looked puzzled. Some were scornful. 'We won't get work', one chirped up, and it was a certainty in his mind. It was my first encounter with an alternative culture.

- **Improving potential earning power**

  Much of further and higher education is focused on achieving this purpose. It involves learning to earn more, to achieve personal wealth, power and status. Much of education at secondary school is also geared towards directing children into careers that not only match their aptitudes and talents but also make them the most money and raise their status.

PRACTICAL TASK

Ask yourself what jobs carry high status in our society. What sort of jobs impress people? Now ask children you know what are the best jobs. They'll probably identify jobs that have a high income with, almost certainly, fame or celebrity attached. The government's long-term goal for at least 50 per cent of adults to get degrees is also part of this acknowledged drive to raise the personal wealth of society's members.

- **Self-realisation, or the realisation of innate potential**

  Ironically, this purpose only emerged in the early Victorian period when Dr Thomas Arnold, who became head of Rugby school, put forward the view that education was for something higher than wealth production and work skills. It was for character building, civilising, producing true Christians and turning boys into gentlemen (a reference to manners, not status). These ideas may seem archaic, but beneath this he felt that schools should help pupils to become the best people they can be. As an idea it appealed greatly in the post-war years after 1918, at least in the minds and hearts of most educators. Today, most of those involved in education directly aspire to this purpose.

PRACTICAL TASK

Spend time now thinking about what purposes our present system of state education would prioritise. Using the table, list those on which our system concentrates and put them in order of most important to least important. Now do this for yourself as an educator. An example has been included.

Education system priorities	My priorities
Work skills	Enjoyment of learning new knowledge and skills

Are your priorities, or the order of them, different from the 'official' ones? If so what difference does that make to your pupils, yourself and the effectiveness of the organisation?

If you would like to read more about this potential conflict of purposes, I recommend reading Wilkins' article 'Is schooling a technology, a process of socialisation, or a consumer product?' in *Management in Education* (2005).

Influences on changes in education provision

We have always taught our children, albeit at home, in the community and at work. The ability and desire of the state to pay for the formal education of children, however, is more subject to fluctuating circumstances and the forces of change. There have been three main groups of forces that have led to change in formal education type and provision. The first group consists of philosophers and educationalists, and to these we can, today, add scientists and psychologists. They reform from within the education system by fundamentally objecting to the existing way of educating, then trying new things and promoting them as better ways. In the past their influence came in convincing practitioners that their system or way of educating was better than conventional practice. Some changes are short-lived, such as the ETA phonics spelling system tried in the 1960s; others are long term, such as the introduction of comprehensive education or co-educational schools (mixed boys and girls).

Currently, concerns from educationalists about the very nature of primary education, in all its aspects, has led to the independent primary education review led by Rob Alexander at Cambridge

University (Primary Review, 2007). Its interim reports have severely criticised the structure, practices and priorities of the present system. In response, the government set up its own primary review led by Jim Rose (DCSF, 2008c) to counteract the impact of such criticism. Guy Claxton (2008) has also just recently published his own critique of the English education system. You might be interested in reading more about what these critics say and judge for yourselves the merits of their cases. Their publication details can be found at the end of this chapter.

The second group of forces centres around those who hold sufficient power to enforce change. Formerly, this would have been kings and queens and the Church, but nowadays this is seen most clearly in central government policy and funding. This is the most obvious driver for change that we currently experience. Consider the new initiatives you are aware of that have been introduced in the last five years. Some are mandatory and universally undertaken, such as *Every Child Matters*, the 14–19 curriculum, the Early Years Foundation Stage, performance management, remodelling the workforce and synthetic phonics. Others are initiatives that tend to be funded only in the short term, but are often universal in their coverage, such as the 'Wave' literacy and numeracy catch-up programmes, 'Lads and Dads' literacy programmes to raise boys' underachievement or learning mentors, although, in this case, schools now self-fund these as they are so effective.

The third group of forces comes from outside the education system. It can best be described as 'outside forces', such as war, economic depression, deep poverty, times of plenty, political doctrine or ideology such as totalitarian states or those influenced by strict application of religious law, and, of great significance for the whole world, the growth of technologies. This last factor will be addressed later, but the others all impact powerfully on education provision and its nature. When we entered the Second World War, children were evacuated from cities, causing overpopulation in rural schools and the initial closure of city schools. Teachers had been enlisted into the armed forces, leaving fewer available nationally. Later, when the children returned to cities, we experienced the Blitz, which decimated school buildings and led to schools running a morning and afternoon school session, with pupils attending either in the morning or afternoon. The schools concentrated on core subjects and PE. There were virtually no resources and no money for repairs and facilities. Classes were large and children were traumatised and exhausted. Contrast that with our provision today and the environment and facilities we have access to. In poorer countries education is a luxury, available only to those who can pay.

REFLECTIVE TASK
Spend a few minutes considering what are the most powerful outside forces affecting your role and setting.

The 'what' of education: past, present and future

One of the ways of anticipating future trends in education is to think about aspects of education provision separately. The curriculum we teach, that is the subjects and subject content, has not remained static. Think back to your own school days. What subjects were you taught in primary and secondary school? I was educated in the 1960s and early 1970s. In primary we had nature walks and French, as well as English, maths and RK (religious knowledge). We did do science but it was taught by listening to the schools radio programme. In my second primary school we only did maths and English in the morning, then the girls did needlework and played rounders, while the boys played football in the afternoons. At secondary school the girls did domestic science and the boys woodwork and metalwork. There was no IT because it didn't exist.

Consider the curriculum today. We've had the application of a compulsory government-determined curriculum since 1988. Science has been elevated to a core subject alongside maths and English, and ICT is also very important. The place of modern foreign languages has been disputed and altered at secondary phase and it will become compulsory at primary level in 2010. Personal, social and health education (PSHE) and citizenship have also made an appearance and, although mostly non-mandatory, their place as a key element of the curriculum is currently being debated (Best, 1999; Crow 2008). The emergence of alternative curricula in Wales and Northern Ireland has added a comparative challenge to the dominance of the English National Curriculum (Aasen and Waters, 2006). We are seeing the growth of metacognition skills work being actively taught, e.g. how to think and solve problems (Claxton, 2002).

You may wish to look at the Steiner Waldorf Schools Fellowship school curriculum. It is very successful but radically different to our own National Curriculum (**www.steinerwaldorf.org**).

PRACTICAL TASK

What will our curriculum in schools look like in 2020? Will it look like your independent school? Will it be very similar to our present one or will there be no 'national curriculum'? Will that have been abandoned in favour of local school, local authority or parental choice? Discuss this with your peers. See if you can predict the future provision.

The how of education: past, present and future

Pedagogy or teaching methods have also been subject to considerable change, particularly with regard to the ideological battle between 'talk and chalk' instructional modes of teaching, promoted by the government-sponsored report by Alexander et al. (1991), and 'facilitation' of learning through independent and pupil initiated activities, currently being reinvigorated as part of the Early Years Foundation Stage. Despite that, good practice has remained fairly constant, based on Galton et al.'s (1990) 'Fitness for Purpose' principle. This argues that teaching well requires the deployment of a mixture of teaching methods at appropriate times.

REFLECTIVE TASK

Think of the last lesson that you observed or in which you participated.

- When, if at all, did the teacher instruct, explain to and question the whole class? (Instructional mode)
- Did the teacher have the pupils undertake group or independent activities? (Facilitation)
- Was there a whole class plenary? (Re-enforcement)

Now think about your own practice.

- What teaching methods did you use?
- Did you explain the task, reword or demonstrate?
- Did you question and observe as tasks were undertaken?
- Did you stop the pupils and explain an issue with which many were having difficulty?
- Did you choose the right methods to achieve the objectives or were you constrained by the environment or prevailing teaching approaches?
- How would you have taught that session ideally?

Future changes in teaching methods may rest with neuroscientific and technological developments. It is in these two fields that we have seen the greatest change of approach, the former with the introduction of methods such as brain gym, VAK (visual, audio, kinaesthetic) learning styles awareness and metacognition or learning power approaches (Claxton, 2002). The latter has led to the use of more internet- and computer-based media, especially the interactive whiteboard, discussed below.

The government has also thrown its weight behind pedagogy reforms. Its future vision rests, among other things, on the development of personalised learning, not by, as teachernet (2005) is at pains to explain, each child having an individually determined curriculum and teacher, but by an increased recognition, by those planning learning, of each child's individual learning needs and styles. This has led to a situation witnessed in one Year 5/6 classroom with 28 pupils, where the numeracy activities were differentiated into 12 separate tasks.

Personalised learning also requires the direct involvement and ownership of the child in their learning by the joint identification of termly and half-termly learning targets in core subjects and, if appropriate, behaviour. In a sense it is the expansion of the SEN system to all pupils. You might already be actively involved in individual target setting and monitoring. It is difficult to argue against this development on principle, but spend some time thinking about the potential constraints on this vision. Is the plan unrealistic or is even partial achievement better than the system we operated before, of large group differentiation and streaming with common objectives and a general pedagogical approach to teaching? You can read more about personalised learning in West-Burnham and Coates (2005).

The where of education: past, present and future

Education doesn't have to take place in a building we would know as a school. Most of our education takes place at home and among our communities. Yet for at least a thousand years pupils have been brought together, initially in monasteries and churches, to be taught. Later, grammar schools were founded for boys. By the late nineteenth century there was a massive expansion of elementary schools to meet the requirements of the Education Act 1870, which made education universally available for all children, boys and girls, between the ages of 5 and 10. The making of universal and free secondary education in 1944 saw a similar expansion of secondary school buildings (Richards, 2006). It is from this legacy that we have our present school buildings, locally provided, reduced in grounds as a result of the playing field 'sell-off' of the 1990s and 2000s and with specialist facilities.

I want to conclude this discussion by considering the possible development of places of education, other than what we would recognise as schools. We have seen the emergence of academies of learning, which, for all the name change, we would recognise as schools, but there are moves to offer a range of alternative settings for learning, such as FE colleges, the workplace and centres such as football clubs, children's centres, home learning and web-based learning in small community cells, based on the models adopted in Finland and Australia, where children are scattered in remote areas.

The drive for alternative settings for education in Britain stems not from geographical difficulties, but social and motivational problems for pupils. More and more parents are educating their children at home because they simply don't feel their children would thrive emotionally or educationally at a school (Freedom for Children to Grow, 2007). Many of the alternative settings are being created as part of the *Every Child Matters* agenda, for children who have become disaffected with the institution we call school. In fairness, this is not just about place, but also about the curriculum, the pace of learning and the social climate of the setting.

There has also been criticism about the large size of schools, especially in secondary settings. There has been successful piloting of big schools splitting up into small sub-schools that are self-contained and share the same staff and spaces, creating smaller, safer and more easily monitored school communities. This is aimed at tackling the pupils' sense of being lost, anonymous and unsafe, as reported in the *Good Childhood* survey (Children's Society, 2006).

If we consider the future of 2020, will we see more use of these alternative venues? Will we see big secondary and primary schools split up organisationally and geographically to support the psychological and safety needs of pupils? If not, what will stop that development? What is your view?

Perhaps it is in the field of technological innovation that the answer to our future education system lies.

E-learning

Education in the twenty-first century will almost certainly involve the exploitation of information and communication technology (ICT) and both teachers and teaching assistants will be required to acquire ICT capability for its effective integration into the classroom. We often hear the word 'e-learning' used and how it can create new learning environments. If someone is using ICT when learning, they are using e-learning. According to the DfES (2003):

> E-learning exploits interactive technologies and communication systems to improve the learning experience. It has the potential to transform the way we teach and learn across the board. It can raise standards, and widen participation in lifelong learning. It cannot replace teachers and lecturers, but alongside existing methods it can enhance the quality and reach of their teaching, and reduce the time spent on administration. It can enable every learner to achieve his or her potential, and help to build an educational workforce empowered to change. It makes possible a truly ambitious education system for a future learning society.

Here are some examples of e-learning:

- a child using an interactive game;
- a pupil using software that has been installed on school computers to complete activities;
- pupils in a geography lesson using computers to complete a virtual field trip.

Why use e-learning?

Becta is the government agency that promotes the effective and innovative use of technology in education. According to Becta (2008):

> We know that technology has the potential to transform learning. We are committed to inspiring education providers to realise that potential, and equip learners for Britain's future success.

Below are some examples of why schools are using e-learning.

- It makes teachers more efficient in preparation, assessment and recording.
- Teachers and teaching assistants can use e-learning to personalise the learning experience for pupils.
- Pupils can access resources at home.
- Pupils can learn at their own pace.
- Lessons can be presented in an exciting way.
- Computer systems can mark work, giving immediate feedback.
- Pupils are not totally reliant on the teacher.
- E-learning can expand the community of learners beyond the classroom.

REFLECTIVE TASK

Think of more examples of e-learning that you have seen in school, and then for each example think of why it was used. Did it improve the learning experience?

ICT and literacy

Some teachers feel that the use of books is more likely to raise standards in English than ICT. Slater (2003), in an article in *The Times Educational Supplement*, accuses Ofsted of being more likely to be impressed by a school's ICT equipment than by its books. Schools spend three times more on ICT than on books, but it is not significant in raising standards. According to Slater, spending on books is more likely to improve pupils' academic performance. According to Johnson (2008), however, in an article in *The Guardian*, statistics that report that reading is on the decline completely fail to consider the amount of reading that we do every day on our computers.

Watson (2002), in his study of schoolbook spending in 1,500 schools, asked teachers to what extent they believed that book stocks are effective in raising standards. The results showed that 90 per cent of primary teachers and 87 per cent of secondary teachers in the study thought that book stocks were effective or highly effective in raising standards. When asked the same question about ICT provision, the results were lower, with 67 per cent of secondary teachers rating it as effective and 50 per cent of primary teachers. It seems that, while most teachers see book stocks as being more effective in raising standards than ICT provision, the majority of teachers feel that ICT also has a part to play in improving academic achievement in English.

Watts and Lloyd (2003), in their paper, 'The use of innovative ICT in the active pursuit of literacy', looked at whether 'Espresso for Schools' (which is a multimedia ICT package) promoted learning. Espresso delivers educational content every week that provides resources for pupils and teachers related to the National Curriculum. It provides television-quality sound and pictures, and the materials for pupils include activities, tasks and games. There is a teacher staffroom to support the materials.

According to Watts and Lloyd, Espresso produced high levels of motivation and helped in the teaching of journalistic writing styles. The pupils found Espresso to be a reliable source of knowledge and information and the teacher was seen as facilitating learning, rather than being the expert provider of information. The learning experience was constructivist in that the teacher did not directly give instructions and there was much pupil autonomy as they developed their written work into a tabloid newspaper form. Graphics and text features helped pupils to present their news articles in a journalistic style. Constructivism is a theory of learning that sees the purpose of learning as a person's construction of his or her own meaning, which focuses on primary concepts, rather than memorising facts. Constructivism is a philosophy of learning founded on the premise that each of us selects our own 'mental models', which we use to make sense of our experiences. We construct new ideas based upon the knowledge we already have, to accommodate new experiences. The teacher should encourage pupils to learn through discovering ideas and knowledge for themselves. Rather than learning the definitions of concepts, they should understand the meaning of them (Novak, 1988).

The research mentions that the software encouraged collaboration, which was ascertained from interviews with teachers and pupils, and observations in the lessons. The key messages from Watts and Lloyd's research are that innovative software can enhance learning, but this may require a different approach to pedagogy with responsibility for learning being devolved from teacher to learner.

Another innovative use of ICT in the pursuit of understanding difficult literacy texts is an educational software known as Kar2ouche, which is a storyboard program designed by collaboration between software designers and professional educators as part of an initiative funded by Intel and based at Oxford University. Kar2ouche and its module 'Macbeth' were evaluated by Peter Birmingham from Oxford University and Chris Davies from 'Immersive Education', who produced the software (Birmingham and Davies, 2001). The purpose of the evaluation was to be formative in order to develop a prototype and then research and develop an understanding of its organisational and cognitive aspects.

Kar2ouche has a storyboarding facility that enables pupils to select images and text from a play, which are all stored on a databank. Pupils can change the direction in which characters face and can change the setting of the scene. In addition, they can change the posture of a character to suggest anger, happiness, etc. The intention is that storyboarding can have an impact on their understanding of text and scenes in the play. Kar2ouche trials took place in three different English classes and the teachers were asked to look at ways in which they could use it to help them achieve their existing aims for studying *Macbeth*. Birmingham and Davies felt it was important that the teachers did not change their existing teaching and learning aims to accommodate the software, and they were asked to accommodate the software into their existing lesson plans.

Birmingham and Davies (2001) believe that the work the pupils were engaged in during the construction of the storyboards is embedded in the conversations that took place between the members of the group. Their research highlights how this software enabled pupils to understand complex language and concepts through interaction between teacher, students and software. The opportunity for collaborative work was not just about taking turns with the mouse and keyboard; instead, Kar2ouche was able to stimulate discussion, focusing on particular scenes and text.

PRACTICAL TASK

List in the table below examples of software used in your school and whether it is passive or whether it involves collaboration and interaction among pupils.

Software	Passive	Collaborative/Interactive
Kar2ouche		✓

Do you think that discourse is important when pupils learn?

Technology and the future

Schools in the future will continue to use e-learning, and technology in education will continue to be promoted as a way to transform learning. Sometimes, when using passive software, pupils remain unchallenged or the lessons can be highly skills oriented. Becker (2000) suggests that teachers should support constructivist pedagogies, rather than a transmission-oriented pedagogy, emphasising group work involving discourse, which goes beyond skills-oriented software. In addition, both Vygotskian and neo-Vygotskian approaches see learning occurring in a social context before becoming internalised, and classwork is achieved collaboratively through interaction among pupils. Discourse is particularly important, as it is the way pupils share experience, through which understandings are constructed (Wegerif and Scrimshaw, 1997).

CHAPTER SUMMARY

- Education appears static and unchanging, but in practice it has always been subject to change and quite fundamental changes at that.
- To understand the structure and nature of education provision, it is important to identify the purposes of education that are dominant at any one time. These include simple survival and the generation of personal and national wealth, global competition, vocational skills development and perpetuating and developing civilised society, as is it perceived by those in charge.
- Change in education provision is often influenced by thinkers and educationalists themselves, political paymasters and outside forces, such as technological and scientific developments, conflict, the state of the economy, nationally, regionally and globally, and political and religious ideologies.
- The future of education will be marked by possible changes in curricula and in teaching methods, including the government's focus on developing personalised learning and meeting the five outcomes of *Every Child Matters*, which it most recently outlined in its visionary document, *The Children's Plan: Building brighter futures* (DCSF, 2008a) and its education-specific follow-up document, *Promoting Excellence for All* (DCSF, 2008b).
- It is that all-encompassing demand for every child to be enabled to learn in a safe, happy and effective way that has led to the consideration of alternative settings other than schools for education.
- In the end, advancing technologies may have the greatest impact on education, in all aspects of delivery; however, the technologies used must remain servants to effective pedagogy and should enhance teaching and learning.
- The future is an exciting and challenging prospect.

REFERENCES

Aasen, W. and Waters, J. (2006) The new curriculum in Wales: a new view of the child? *Education 3–13*, 34(2): 123–9.

Aldrich, R. (1982) *An Introduction to the History of Education*. London: Hodder and Stoughton.

Alexander, J., Rose, J. and Woodhead, C. (1992) *Curriculum Organisation and Classroom Practice in Primary Schools*. London: DES.

Becker, H.J. (2000) *Findings from the Teaching, Learning, and Computing Survey: Is Larry Cuban right?* Revision of a paper written for the School Technology Leadership Conference of the Council of Chief State School Officers, Washington, DC, January. Available online at www.crito.uci.edu/tlc/findings/ccsso.pdf (accessed 11 August 2008).

Becta (2008) *About Becta*. Available online at http://about.becta.org.uk/display.cfm?page=1616 (accessed 18 August 2008).

Best, R. (1999) Pastoral care and the millennium, in Collins, U. and McNiff, J. (eds) *Rethinking Pastoral Care*. London: Routledge.

Birmingham, P. and Davies, C. (2001) Storyboarding Shakespeare: learners' interactions with storyboard software in the process of understanding difficult literacy texts. *Journal of Information Technology for Teacher Education*, 10(3). Available online at http://students. ced.appstate.edu/newmedia/06chort/morrisey/5200/mod1/shakespear.pdf (accessed 8 July 2008).

Children's Society (2006) *Good Childhood? A question for our times.* Available online at www.goodchildhood.org.uk (accessed 13 August 2008).

Claxton, G. (2002) *Building Learning Power: Helping young people to become better learners.* London: TLO.

Claxton, G. (2008) *What's the Point of School? Rediscovering the heart of education*. London: Oneworld.

Crow, F. (2008) Learning for well-being: personal, social and health education and the changing curriculum. *Pastoral Care in Education*, 26(1): 43–51.

Department for Children, Schools and Families (DCSF) (2005) *Higher Standards, Better Schools for All: More choice for parents and pupils*. London: TSO.

Department for Children, Schools and Families (DCSF) (2008a) *The Children's Plan: Building brighter futures*. London: TSO.

Department for Children, Schools and Families (DCSF) (2008b) *Promoting Excellence for All. School Improvement Strategy: Raising standards, supporting schools*. London: TSO.

Department for Children, Schools and Families (DCSF) (2008c) *Independent Review of the Primary Curriculum.* Available online at www.dcsf.gov.uk/primarycurriculumreview (accessed 13 August 2008).

Department for Education and Employment/Qualifications and Curriculum Authority (DfEE/QCA) (1999) *The National Curriculum, Key Stages 1 and 2*. London: HMSO. Available online at http://curriculum.qca.org.uk/uploads/Statement-of-values_tcm8–12166.pdf (accessed 7 August 2008).

Department for Education and Skills (DfES) (2003) *Towards a Unified e-Learning Strategy*. Available online at: www.dcsf.gov.uk/consultations/conResults.cfm?consultationId=774 (accessed 11 August 2008).

Freedom for Children to Grow (2007) *The Home Education Campaign.* Available online at www.freedomforchildrentogrow.org/ (accessed 13 August 2008).

Galton, M., Simon, B. and Croll, P. (1990) *Inside the Primary Classroom.* London: Routledge.

Johnson, S. (2008) *Dawn of the Digital Natives: Is reading declining?* Available online at www.guardian.co.uk/technology/2008/feb/07/internet.literacy (accessed 11 August 2008).

Novak, J. (1998) *Learning, Creating and Using Knowledge.* Mahwah, NJ: Lawrence Erlbaum Associates.

Primary Review (2007) *The Condition and Future of Primary Education in England.* Available online at www.primaryreview.org.uk (accessed 13 August 2008).

Richards, C. (2006) The establishment of English primary education 1941–1946. *Pastoral Care in Education*, 34(1): 5–10.

Slater, J. (2003) Books lose their appeal. *Times Educational Supplement*, 26 September.

teachernet (2005) *Personalised Learning.* Available online at www.teachernet.gov.uk/personalisedlearning(accessed 13 August 2008).

Watson, R. (2002) *Schoolbook Spending in the UK 2001/2002*. London: Educational Publishers Council.

Watts, M. and Lloyd, C. (2004) The use of innovative ICT in the active pursuit of literacy. *Journal of Computer Assisted Learning*, 20: 50–8.

Wegerif, R. and Scrimshaw, P. (1997) *Computer and Talk in the Primary Classroom*. Clevedon: Multilingual Matters.

West-Burnham, J. and Coates, M. (2005) *Personalizing Learning*. London: Continuum.

Wilkins, R. (2005) Is schooling a technology, a process of socialisation, or a consumer product? *Management in Education*, 19(1): 25–31.

FURTHER READING

Carnell, E. (2004) *It's Like Mixing Colours: How young people view their learning within the context of the Key Stage Three National Strategy*. London: ATL.

Dent, H.C. (1982) *Education in England and Wales*. London: Hodder and Stoughton.

HM Treasury/DCSF (2007) *Aiming High for Young People: A ten year strategy for positive activities*. London: TSO.

Holmes-Beck, R. (1965) *A Social History of Education*. New York: Prentice Hall.

Newby, M. (2005) *A Learners' Curriculum: Towards a curriculum for the twenty-first century*. London: ATL.

APPENDIX: GLOSSARY OF ABBREVIATIONS

ADD	attention deficit disorder
ADHD	attention deficit hyperactivity disorder
APA	annual performance assessment
ASD	autistic spectrum disorder
BIP	behaviour improvement programmes
CAF	Common Assessment Framework
CAMHS	Child and Adolescent Mental Health Service
CD	conduct disorder
CPD	continuing professional development
CSIE	Centre for Studies on Inclusive Education
CVC	consonant, vowel, consonant
DCSF	Department for Children, Schools and Families
DES	Department of Education and Science
DfEE	Department for Education and Employment
DfES	Department for Education and Skills
ECM	Every Child Matters
EPPI	Evidence for Policy and Practice Information
EYFS	Early Years Foundation Stage
FE	further education
FSA	family support assistant
GPC	Grapheme–Phoneme Correspondence

HLTA	Higher Level Teaching Assistant
ICT	information and communication technology
IEP	Individual Education Plan
IQ	intelligence quotient
IQF	Integrated Qualifications Framework
IT	information technology
JAR	joint area review
LSA	learning support assistant
MLD	moderate learning difficulties
NCL	National College for School Leadership
NEET	not in education, employment or training
NLS	National Literacy Strategy
NNS	National Numeracy Strategy
NPSLBA	National Programme for Specialist Leaders of Behaviour and Attendance
NRT	National Remodelling Team
NUT	National Union of Teachers
OCD	obsessive compulsive disorder
ODD	oppositional defiance disorder
Ofsted	Office for Standards in Education
PE	physical education
PPA	planning, preparation and assessment
PSHE	personal, social and health education
PSP	Pastoral Support Programme
QCA	Qualifications and Curriculum Authority
RE	religious education
RK	religious knowledge
SEAL	social and emotional aspects of learning
SENCO	Special Educational Needs Co-ordinator
SpLD	specific learning difficulties
SSA	special support assistant
TA	teaching assistant
TDA	Training and Development Agency
TES	*Times Educational Supplement*
UNESCO	United Nations Educational, Scientific, and Cultural Organization
VAK	visual, audio, kinaesthetic
VC	vowel, consonant
WAMG	Workforce Agreement Monitoring Group
WIIFM	What's in it for me?

Index